Without Consent

The Blazer Lectures for 1987

Without Consent

MASS-ELITE LINKAGES
IN PRESIDENTIAL POLITICS

Warren E. Miller

THE UNIVERSITY PRESS OF KENTUCKY

Library of Congress Cataloging-in-Publication Data

Miller, Warren E. (Warren Edward), 1924-
  Without consent : mass-elite linkages in presidential politics /
Warren E. Miller.

      p. cm. — (The Blazer lectures ; 1987)
  Bibliography: p.
  Includes index.
  ISBN 0-8131-0550-1
  1. Political conventions—United States. 2. Primaries—United
States. 3. Elite (Social sciences) 4. Presidents—United States—
Election. 5. Representative government and representation—United
States. I. Title. II. Series.
JK2063.M55 1988
324.5'0973—dc19   88-3217

Contents

Tables

Foreword

Intellectual and artistic pursuits have long benefited from the generosity and support of members of society who have recognized the importance of curiosity, exploration, and the search for new ideas and new knowledge. The University of Kentucky has been fortunate to have shared in the generosity offered by a large number of the Commonwealth's citizens. The Blazer Lecture Series, supported since 1949 by the Paul G. and Georgia M. Blazer Fund, is an example of this contribution to the intellectual life of the faculty and students at the university and to the surrounding community. In the almost four decades since the Blazer Lecture Series was founded, the University of Kentucky has been able to present such distinguished speakers as Henry Steele Commager, the noted historian; Barry Bingham, Sr., of the Louisville *Courier Journal*; Henry Cabot Lodge, ambassador and senator; and President Gerald Ford.

The continued generosity and interest of the Blazer family have allowed us in recent years to have as lecturers Dr. William DeVries, noted heart surgeon, and Dr. Daniel Boorstin, Librarian of Congress. Now, beginning with the lectures delivered in the spring of 1987, the College of Arts and Sciences at the university, in cooperation with the University Press of Kentucky, is pleased to be able to share these lectures through the publication of an annual monograph.

The 1987 Blazer Lectures were given by Dr. Warren E. Miller at the Lexington campus on March 9 and 10, 1987, as part of a conference on Ideology and Polarization in American Politics. Dr. Miller is professor of political science at Arizona State University, a former president of the American Political Science Association, and director of one of the most respected on-going collections of social science data in the United States, the National Election Studies.

The College of Arts and Sciences is pleased to share the ideas of such a noted scholar through our first Blazer Lecture monograph. Our pleasure is doubled by the thought that we are fortunate enough to have the support of three generations of a distinguished Kentucky family who recognize the importance of intellectual pursuits in the humanities and the social sciences.

Michael A. Baer, Dean
College of Arts and Sciences
University of Kentucky

Preface

The exploration of public attitudes is a pursuit of endless
fascination—and frustration. Depiction of the distribution
of opinions within the public, identification of the qualities of opinion, isolation of the odd and of the obvious
correlates of opinion, and ascertainment of the modes of
opinion formation are pursuits that excite human curiosity. Yet these endeavors are bootless (for the political
scientist) unless the findings about the preferences, aspirations, and prejudices of the public can be connected
with the workings of the governmental system.—V.O.
Key, Jr., *Public Opinion and American Democracy* (1961)

In the concluding chapter of *Public Opinion and American
Democracy*, V.O. Key, Jr., thus anticipated the motive for
writing *Without Consent*. Key spent a fruitful and influential
year with us at the Survey Research Center in 1959-1960. In
that year he set aside the embryonic work that was posthu-
mously published as *The Responsible Electorate*, did a begin-
ning-to-end editing of the manuscript for *The American Voter*,
persuaded Miller and Stokes to make the constituency, not
constituents, the unit of analysis for their "forthcoming" work
on congressional representation, and began what was to be the
last major work of his career, *Public Opinion and American
Democracy*. Although we at Michigan were already striving
to place our own work on mass electoral behavior in the tradition identified with Lippmann and Key, Key's presence did
much to affirm our intention to move to studies of the interaction and interdependence of various separable components
of the political process.

In the ensuing years we actually made only limited attempts to reach beyond the American voter at home, although many of us participated in studies of mass-elite linkages and interactions in other polities, particularly in western Europe. But in 1972, the Center for Political Studies undertook the first of what have now been three national data collections focused exclusively on American political elites. In 1973, 1981, and 1985 senior staff members of the Center carried out more or less elaborate post-election studies of delegates to the national nominating conventions of both major political parties.

The present volume is the third in a sequence reporting this research done by the Center. The series of books was inaugurated with Jeane Kirkpatrick's volume on political elites, a book focused on the rise of *The New Presidential Elite* in 1972. The next in the sequence, ten years later, was the Miller/Jennings volume that presented the presidential *Parties in Transition. Without Consent* is a sequel to the first two. But it is less a "part of an unfolding series" or a "natural consequence" of the first two, than a direct product of the general line of thought associated with scholars from Lippmann to Key who have been concerned with the connection between public opinion and democracy.

Without Consent adds to the portfolio of work Key deemed essential to answer the "fundamental question of how it is that democratic governments manage to operate at all." It really fits in a sequel of learning first about the citizenry, then about the elite, and finally about their interaction. In Key's words, writing in 1960:

Analytically it is useful to conceive of the structure of a democratic order as consisting of the political activists and the mass of people. . . . The data [pertaining to citizens' attitudes] tell us almost nothing about the dynamic relations between the upper layer of activists and mass opinion. The missing piece of our puzzle is this elite element of the opinion system. That . . . political influentials both affect mass opinion and are conditioned in their behavior by it is obvious. Yet systematic knowledge of the composition, distribution in the social structure, and patterns of behavior of this sector of the political system remains far from satisfactory.

The longer one frets with the puzzle of how democratic regimes manage to function, the more plausible it appears that a substantial part of the explanation is to be found in the motives that actuate the leadership echelon, the values that it holds, in the rules of the political game to which it adheres . . . and perhaps in some of the objective circumstances, both personal and institutional, in which it functions.[2]

Without Consent offers a limited view of elite motives and values, but it explores more extensively than most studies the impact of the rules of the game and the consequences of objective circumstances for the linkage of mass and elite policy preferences. Although it is difficult to reconstruct even perceived causal influences, there is little question but that close contact with V.O. Key at the time of our writing *The American Voter*, the first analyses from the Miller/Stokes study of congressional representation, and of the first drafts of *Public Opinion and American Democracy* fixed the concern with mass-elite linkages as a part of my personal research agenda. Even more, Key's preoccupation with reintroducing politics and political institutions into the micro-analysis of political behavior reaffirmed an earlier conviction that the behavioral mode could address many topics of political analysis central to understanding the actual functioning of a democratic system of politics and government.

Without Consent is only a limited instance of the empirical study of mass-elite linkages embedded in the processes of electoral politics and democratic government in the United States. I hope that it will be followed by other studies of elite-mass interactions in other settings.

To whatever degree the book represents progress toward Key's goal, it also represents the indispensable contribution of a host of colleagues. First and foremost it reflects the insights into the nature of politics and research on politics provided by

Kent Jennings and Barbara Farah. All three of us participated in the design of the 1981 and 1985 studies. Barbara directed the collection of data in 1981 and provided invaluable consultation on the execution of the 1985 data collection. The direct responsibility for that collection was in the hands of Debra Dodson, now research associate at the Center for the American Woman in Politics, Rutgers University. The data, along with those from 1972 and 1980, are all available for further analysis through the Inter-University Consortium for Political and Social Research at the University of Michigan.

As will become evident to the reader, the analytic mode of this book was anticipated in *Parties in Transition*, written with M. Kent Jennings. Indeed, had our work schedules not dictated otherwise, the present volume would have benefited from Kent's continuing interest in the study of political elites and mass-elite linkages. Absent that contribution, *Without Consent* is still the beneficiary of his central role in both the 1981 and the 1985 studies.

Building on Debra Dodson's preparation of data files, David Malin, graduate assistant in the Political Science Department at Arizona State University, responded to the innumerable curiosities that precede a large-scale data analysis and produced a host of imaginative and yet precise manipulations of the data. His diligence and efficiency ultimately made it possible to carry out complete replications of a large-scale data management project, using both the 1981 and the 1985 data collections, in a remarkably short time. Thanks to his tenacity and his understanding of a great many specific analytic objectives, I am confident that the analytic shortcomings of the book are mine in concept, not his in execution.

Given my slightly antiquarian work ways, the real challenge en route to the final manuscript was provided by my penchant for oral dictation or indecipherable handwriting. Linda Morgan coped with both with good humor and great efficiency, aided by Nancy Brennan and Judy Ottmar. Their work, in turn, was followed by the manifold contributions of the University Press of Kentucky.

All of us were supported in our joint endeavor by a number of sponsoring institutions. The Russell Sage Foundation made the initial contribution with a grant that underwrote a large fraction of the costs of data collection. The balance of those costs, along with others entailed in data preparation, were carried by the Center for Political Studies. The third of the inadvertent partners was my home institution, Arizona State University, which made it possible for Linda Morgan, David Malin, and me to complete a complicated but rewarding task in record time. As Dean Baer's Foreward indicates, the University of Kentucky and the Blazer family fund were partners in an indispensable fourth source of support.

Finally, a fifth institution, that of marriage, provided a wife whose contributions were only grudgingly those of the mundane connubial order, but most generously those of a professional colleague. As a student of politics, research scholar, and teacher, she provided not only helpful consultation and insightful advice but reassurance that the final product at least warranted the strain that writing always imposes on our many other institutional relationships.

1

Introduction: The Study of Presidential Politics in America

As the end of the twentieth century approaches, the more cynical of the commentators describing the political American scene are prone to repeat the caricature of the American presidential selection process as the "selling of a president." With politics entering the era of high technology in mass communications, the serious process of democratic self-government is often portrayed as one involving only the imagemakers, two or more malleable candidates for an elective office, and the gullible electorate. In the early days of each election-year cycle, "name recognition" and trial heat comparisons of candidate popularity are the name of the game, and the role of the campaign consultant in the packaging of candidates scarcely diminishes before the ultimate first Tuesday.

Nevertheless, it takes little in the way of close observation to understand that much more is involved in our national politics than the personal popularity of candidates for public office. One need only note the hundreds of millions of dollars contributed to election campaign funding to conclude that a great many individual contributors think the outcome will make a very substantial practical difference. Those who finance politics apparently recognize that whatever one's philosophy about the desirable level of governmental intervention in the everyday lives of citizens, the world of the late twentieth century is inevitably one in which *either* action *or* inaction on the part of our government can make a very real difference in determining who within the society receives what rewards.

The extensive literature reporting systematic analyses of mass electoral behavior supports the inference that this conclusion is shared by millions of voters. Between the early 1950s and the late 1980s, the quality of mass electoral decision-making underwent marked change. It would be going too far to say that issue voting came to dominate the voters' choices; however, the evidence does suggest that the net outcome of most of the elections of the 1970s and 1980s was determined by voters' policy preferences and their assessment of incumbents' performance in office.[1]

With the advent of television and the evolution of modern campaign technology, citizen responses to the problems of self-government have changed dramatically during the four decades following World War II. Although the war clearly intruded on many aspects of American national development, the full-scale renewal of national politics after the war largely extended, unchanged, the party-dominated politics of the immediate pre-war period. Eisenhower's first election was notable because of the personal presence of a national hero, but his presidency did little to alter the dominant role of party in shaping electoral decisions. Thirty years later, however, candidates had challenged parties as the focus of voter interests. Nowhere was this more true than in the domain of issue voting.

In the first Eisenhower-Stevenson contest, voters' concerns about policy were almost always expressed in their evaluation of the political parties, virtually never in popular assessments of the presidential candidates. By the late 1970s that had all changed; it was the candidates, not the parties, who were associated with issue preferences.[2] With the parties no longer the ubiquitous guide, helping the voter transform concerns with either domestic or foreign problems into policy preferences and hence electoral choices, the process of casting a vote rooted in policy preferences became more and more complex.

There was no diminution of popular concern with issues of

the day but rather a shift in the basis upon which voters made their choices. Indeed, by the 1980s it was commonplace for the political analyst and commentator to note that national decisions at the polls were heavily influenced, even dominated, by voters' assessments of presidential performance. Not only were presidential approval ratings the stuff of daily news analysis and speculation, but in every election from the Goldwater-Johnson contest on, presidential performance and the judgments levied on each incumbent administration provided a major explanation for the determination of the White House's next occupant.[3] Although party, in the form of the voter's self-identified partisanship, continued to be the most important single determinant of voters' choices, policy preferences and performance evaluations associated with presidential contenders were of undeniable importance in election results in the 1980s; this was particularly evident in the election and reelection of Ronald Reagan.

The utility of this book rests in substantial part on the conclusion that policies and issues, and their symbolic representations, play a major role in the determination of national electoral outcomes. And even if party remains the most salient single cue for the issue voter, while the relevance of candidate-based factionalism waxes and wanes, issues have a continuing generic importance in their own right in the American process of selecting a president. Consequently, it is neither simply an old-fashioned adherence to notions of responsible party government nor fear of the "mischiefs of faction" that motivates concern with the linkages connecting the policy preferences of the mass electorate to the authoritative decisions of the leaders.

This book gives short shrift to the study of candidates' personalities and personal images. It does not even have much to say about the origins of partisan differentiation with regard to the issue preferences of the voters. This is not a book on voting behavior. It does attend to the relative importance of party, issues, and candidate, but is primarily concerned with the circumstances which enhance or inhibit the sharing of policy pref-

erences and related symbolic attitudes among leaders and
followers in American society.

The Objective of the Study

This study is an inquiry into some of the ways in which the
authoritative allocation of values through decisions taken near
the peak of the pyramid of political power come to reflect the
predispositions and preferences of the mass electorate that
makes up the pyramid's base.

However old-fashioned the metaphor of the pyramid of
power, it does provide a useful image of the structured manner
in which popular power in a democratic society is connected
to a handful of individuals who ultimately make and implement
governmental decisions in the name of popular sovereignty. In
our rough translation of the metaphor, the broad base of the
pyramid is provided by the tens of millions of citizens who
are eligible to participate in the electoral process. The voters,
in turn, can be arrayed in successive strata ranging from relatively indifferent participants to those who are more and more
intensely involved in the electoral process. As one moves above
the broadest base, made up of voters who are otherwise inactive
in politics, to those who are informal participants in the campaign and then on to formally defined activists, the numbers
associated with each stratum shrink rapidly. Immediately above
the upper levels of informal rank-and-file participants are the
strata made up of those members of the elite who populate
local power constellations—precinct and ward politicians, contenders for local office, and those who occupy the organizational positions in the townships, towns, and cities—followed
by county and then state activists. Near the top are the more
rarefied strata of those preoccupied with national and, ultimately, presidential politics.

As with most metaphors, the limited usefulness of the pyramid image becomes more and more apparent as one tries to

draw into it more and more systematic information. We know that many voters are not much interested in national politics; therefore, we cannot presume that the mass base is really a homogeneous foundation for the rest of the pyramid. Moving vertically up the axis of the pyramid, however, one presumably encounters larger and larger proportions of smaller and smaller strata whose members are more and more preoccupied with presidential politics. In fact, little is known about the empirical regularities that integrate or differentiate lower and middle and upper elites along dimensions of status, power, activity, and national focus.

In any event, the political process of choosing the nation's leaders clearly involves hundreds of thousands of citizens who make up a political mid-elite that plays a vital role throughout the entire presidential selection process. This study is particularly concerned with those in the upper reaches of the pyramid who are most deeply involved in the mobilization and allocation of resources in the early stages. It is centered on the universe of sometime convention delegates who typically precede, and subsequently follow, their stints as nominators with roles as presidential campaign activists.

Given the origins of this program of research on convention delegates, it would be less than forthright to pretend that those of us involved in the investigation deliberately chose to study delegates as the ideal representatives of political elites. Nonetheless, this inquiry (as well as the earlier study reported in *Parties in Transition*)[4] was prompted by the belief that delegates who have been or later become campaign activists are exceptionally important contributors to subsequent decisions by nominated candidates—and elected presidents—concerning matters of public policy. We believe that they include many influentials who participate in shaping subsequent Administration policy. In the role of political influentials they link the president and his office to the partisan base that provided electoral support at the polls.

In the absence of systematic evidence on the point, we would argue, alternatively, that delegate campaigners may be the president's analogue of the congressman's "primary constituency" as defined and described by Richard Fenno.[5] In that role they would be less important as independent contributors to policy decisions but more important as the presumed representatives of the public opinion that links the candidate and the candidate's mass base of popular support. As participants in presidential politics who have some base of local support, they may be used by the inner circles of leadership as the sounding board for public opinion.

This inquiry is not directed at determining the extent to which convention delegates actually play these imputed roles. Such a study should have a high place on the priority list for future research, but it has not yet been done and is no part of this book. Therefore I presume, but do not demonstrate, that as political activists in community, state, and nation, those who have come to our attention for other reasons connect the top and the bottom of the pyramid of political power in ways that go well beyond the episodes that are the presidential elections themselves—in short, that the universe of convention elites is made up of political actors who are of continuing importance to the ongoing politics of the nation.[6]

Since the advent of survey research as an integrated collection of methods for large-scale social inquiry, more attention has been given to the nature of the base of the political pyramid than to those elements that connect the base to the apex. Indeed, mass electoral behavior is too often taken to define the essence of presidential politics. There are, of course, notable exceptions: some scholars with a grand sweep cover the whole range of actors and activities that make up the presidential parties;[7] others concentrate on the organizational infrastructure of political parties.[8] A few produce sophisticated syntheses of the entire process and separate the central phenomena from the often more colorful epiphenomena.[9] Nevertheless, it is the voters who have received the most persistent scrutiny, with large-scale programmatic studies mounted every biennium to depict the values and beliefs, hopes and fears, that lead to citizens' decisions to participate—or not—on behalf of a particular candidate or set of party candidates.

Perhaps because of the costs and logistic challenges confronting comparable inquiries into the study of political elites, there has been only a limited, if growing, accretion of information about them. It has been still rarer to have research resources concentrated on an inquiry into the nature of the interconnectedness of the mass base of presidential politics and a population of partisan activists.[10] This book is directed at the latter task; it is about some of the institutions that link the issue preferences and ideological predispositions of rank-and-file citizens to the preferences or predispositions of the mid-level leaders of the presidential parties. As already noted, this is *not* a book primarily about the process of choosing a president; it is therefore not directly about decisions in elections or about nominating conventions. Although it may have many implications for our understanding of the dynamics of these and other institutions that contribute to the political process, it is essentially a static analysis of some of the more persistent similarities and differences that unite or divide two strata of participants.

This study is one of similarities and differences in ideological predispositions that are reflected when ordinary citizens *and* mid-level political elites locate themselves as liberal, moderate, or conservative participants in partisan politics—where they are also identified as Republicans and Democrats. It is a book about the congruence of policy or issue preferences among the masses and the elites as those preferences are central to the disagreements between presidential parties or among party factions. It is about agreement and disagreement in attitudes toward the political groups that have come to symbolize the political values that are controlled by the authoritative acts of government. The book is not about the evolution of these predispositions, preferences, or attitudes toward symbolic groups; it is about political circumstances and conditions that appear to enhance or inhibit similarities in such predispositions and preferences among political elites and ordinary citizens. Because our elites are made up of sometime delegates to national nominating conventions, and because the national conventions are institutionalized occasions for representatives of the mass population to participate—however directly or indirectly—in the presidential selection process, the book is about representation. I will have more to say about the delegates' roles as self-conscious representatives of mass opinion; for the moment, it is enough to note that not much of the literature analyzing delegates to nominating conventions considers their representation of anything other than support for candidates.[11] Indeed, some of the critics of the party reforms of the 1970s have castigated delegates who declare some purpose *other* than that of choosing the party standard-bearer who is most likely to produce electoral victory in November. Nonetheless, the very concept of mass-elite linkage used here is precisely intended to address the interconnectedness of political attitudes that constitute at least part of the content of political representation.

The Setting and Design of the Study

The portion of this investigation dealing with political elites was preceded by two earlier and related inquiries. The first was launched in 1972, billed as a study of women in American politics. After some two years of discussion and planning, the two national party nominating conventions of that year were selected as sites for what was expected to be the first of a series of national studies of the emergence of women as full participants in national politics. Although the 1972 study was a thoroughgoing intellectual, organizational, and technical success—four senior scholars collaborated in designing and executing a complex and marvelously rich set of data collections— very little was learned that was unique to new roles for women in politics. Instead, a great deal was learned about the people Jeane Kirkpatrick named "The New Presidential Elite."[12]

After an eight-year lapse, a sequel to the 1972 data collection was completed following the 1980 elections. The two data collections were used as the basis for a second volume which built on the tradition begun by McClosky in 1956 when his study of convention delegates was used to analyze mass-elite agreements on questions of public policy preference.[13] This second volume, *Parties in Transition*, also picked up Kirkpatrick's interest in the circulation of political elites and a corollary interest in party factionalism.[14]

The present study of delegates to the 1984 conventions, more than either earlier study, was designed with the present analysis of mass-elite linkages clearly in mind. This was feasible because of the well-established and funded plans for the 1984 National Election Study of the mass electorate.

The plan to use the 1984 study of convention delegates as a vehicle for explorations of mass-elite linkages was not unique to the data collections that provide the primary base for this book. A substantial section on mass-elite relationships was central to our report based on the 1972 and 1980 data collections. Indeed, the early analyses for that volume led us to anticipate with greater clarity the need for complementarity in the 1984 data collections. The present volume is the product of that planning.

The data were produced by a self-administered questionnaire mailed to a universe of convention delegates that included all participants in the earlier two studies as well as delegates to the 1984 conventions. The questionnaire was assembled with the well-defined plans for the issue content of the 1984 National Election Study (NES) of the electorate clearly in mind. The consequence of this anticipation is a substantially enriched array of completely comparable data for both the sample of the mass electorate and the universe of convention delegates.

Of course, in order to take maximum advantage of the opportunity to do a 1984 study of mass-elite linkages pertaining to policy, we had to design the delegate study content to match the issue content of the 1984 election campaign as reflected in the 1984 NES study. The cost of that closer integration was a considerable *discontinuity* between the specific issue and policy content of the 1980 and 1984 studies of convention delegates.

Our 1980 delegate study had permitted us to examine five different sets of items measuring political attitudes: a single-item measure of ideological self-designation (liberal, moderate, conservative); a five-item liberal/conservative index of policy preferences; and three indices of attitudes toward politically relevant groups, including six "New Left" groups, five traditional political groups, and two groups central to the new themes of moral assessment. Given the need for data to meet other study objectives, the match with 1980 NES data was only partial, and the five measures became three when we turned our attention to the relationship between attitudes of party elites and party followers.

Because the content for the 1984 delegate study was shaped by independent decisions defining the content of the NES survey of the electorate, there are only eight discrete items (embedded in four of the five 1980 indices) that are directly comparable in the 1980 and 1984 mass-elite studies. On the other hand, the 1984 measures rest on a somewhat larger array of items quite strictly comparable on both the elite and the mass level. The bulk of the 1984 analysis rests on the same single-item indicator of ideological predisposition and five multi-item measures of policy preference or symbolic political values. The single-item self-designation of ideological position provides direct continuity with 1980. A second measure is based on a combination of social-issue questions touching on race, gender, and moral issues, such as abortion and gender equality. As a direct counterpart, a third indicator reflects attitudes toward various New Politics groups concerned with the new social issues: the Moral Majority, gay rights groups, the women's movement, and Blacks. A fourth measure, focusing on foreign policy and defense, is a composite of attitudes on three questions of public policy central to the 1984 election. The fifth examines domestic issues in a series of six questions pertaining to desired spending levels for such domestic programs as health, education, and science and technology. The sixth is an indicator of political values resting once more on attitudes toward politically relevant groups—this time, groups involved in traditional party politics: labor unions, business interests, Democrats and Republicans, liberals and conservatives. The composition of the six measures is specified in Appendix B.

The interpretation of our data analyses in 1984 was facilitated by the strict comparability of measurement procedures followed in assessing each of these six indicators of politically relevant values both at the mass and the elite level. Substantial care was taken to ensure that both rank-and-file members of the electorate and the members of our political elite were asked precisely the same questions or exposed to the same stimuli. Each measure of preferences in a given policy domain is based on the same set of items for both populations of political actors. To facilitate comparisons among the composite indicators, each indicator, as well as the ideological self-designation item, has been transformed alternative to 100 as the most conservative score.

In sum, our measures of ideological predispositions, issue preferences, and attitudes toward symbolic political groups were created in highly comparable fashion for the entire election studies sample of the 1984 electorate and for the universe of activists who were delegates in 1980 or 1984 *and* who were active participants in the 1984 presidential campaign. With the 1984 study as a base line for comparison, we have reconstructed all the measures from the 1980 data collections and have carried out parallel analyses for the 1980 and 1984 delegates who were activists in 1980 and the 1980 NES national sample of citizens.

In the original 1980 delegate analysis, presented in *Parties in Transition*, the ideological structure of American presiden-

Table 1. Mean Scores on Issue Index, 1980

	Elite Candidate Preference Groups					Mass
	DEMOCRATS					
Issue index	22	29	35	44	47	49
Number of cases	295	602	295	610	178	842
	REPUBLICANS					
Issue index	61	—	70	—	81	59
Number of cases	386	—	184	—	571	527

Source: Warren E. Miller and M. Kent Jennings, *Parties in Transition* (New York: Russell Sage Foundation, 1986), 226, 228.

Index scores range from 0 (liberal) to 100 (conservative). See *Parties in Transition* for definitions of the candidate preference groups.

tial politics was observed to be strongly affected by three sets of elements common to the structure of electoral competition. The first and most important of the sets is made up of the two political parties as each is represented on both mass and elite levels. Interparty differences on both levels were observed in 1980 and reassessed in 1984. The 1980 observations were then extended to include *intra*party differences created by factional competition within the elites in the struggles for party leadership and nomination. The candidate preferences of the elite participants in the campaigns are thus treated as a second set of variation in linkages between political activists and political supporters. The third is found in the circulation of the political elites. The present analysis seeks further evidence that mobilization and disengagement contribute to the waxing and waning of both intra- and interparty differences.

The extent of differentiation, both within and between parties, is well represented by Table 1, which depicts mean scores on the composite issue index used in the 1980 study. Given the patterns of candidate preference across the three elections of 1972, 1976, and 1980, it was possible to discern five major candidate factions within the active Democratic elite in 1980.

As the table indicates, factional mean scores on the issue index ranged from a liberal 22 for the "left wing" of the Democratic party (roughly represented by the pattern of McGovern-Udall-Kennedy preferences) to a score of 47 represented by former Carter supporters who opted out of campaign activity in 1980. All five factions were visibly, if not always significantly, more liberal than the Democratic rank-and-file, which had a mean score of 49 on the same issue index. The mean score of Republican counterparts in the mass electorate was a full ten points higher—that is, more conservative—and their mean position, in turn, was slightly more liberal than the most liberal of the Republican elite factions (made up of those who preferred someone other than Reagan in both 1976 and 1980). The gap between this representation of the most liberal Republican wing (with a score of 61) and the stalwart conservative faction, made up of those who preferred Reagan both years (scoring 81), was virtually as great as that between the left and the right wings of the Democratic party.

Without repeating and updating the earlier analysis, the impact of the third factor influencing mass elite linkages can be seen in Table 2. As of the 1980 campaign, the circulating elements of the Democratic elite had produced a small drift to the right simply through its changing composition. Our rather detailed analysis of both net and gross estimates of change among the Democrats argues that the move to the right did not result simply from the high rate of disengagement of McGovern and Udall supporters; in fact, those in their ranks who did drop out after the 1972 election were among the more conservative, not the more liberal, of their numbers. The Democratic move to the right occurred because those who were mobilized after the 1972 election, particularly for Carter's nomination in 1976, were more conservative than the continuing core of activists whom they joined in the 1980 campaign, or even the relatively conservative dropouts whom they replaced.

A quite different consequence of elite circulation appeared among Republicans: there, the drift to the right that paralleled

Table 2. Mean Scores on Issue Index, 1980, for Circulating
Components of Party Elites

	Mobilized after 1972	Continuously Active 1972-80	Disengaged after 1972
Democrats	40	35	37
Number of cases	338	1344	415
Republicans	74	73	64
Number of cases	208	1088	140

Source: Warren E. Miller and M. Kent Jennings, *Parties in Transition*
(New York: Russell Sage Foundation, 1986), 137.

Index scores range from 0 (liberal) to 100 (conservative). Definitions of
circulating components may be found in *Parties in Transition*, Table 2.3,
p. 36.

the net move on the Democratic side was produced almost
entirely by the disengagement of the more liberal among the
Republican elite. The net result was a continuation of the polarization of partisan elites that had been developing over the
preceding eight years.

We are short on directly comparable data for earlier years,
but we would not expect a broader historical sweep to indicate
that the period of the 1980s is spectacularly unique. Certainly
intraparty differences among both Democrats and Republicans
have often been noted in the past. And despite those who
sometimes characterize the American two-party system as the
politics of Tweedledum and Tweedledee, there has long been
evidence that persistent party differences of substantial magnitude have shaped our national political contests.[15]

2

Partisan Polarization
and Factionalism,
1980 and 1984

First interpretations of the 1984 Reagan landslide concluded
that the election had produced a mandate for continuation of
the national shift to the right on matters of ideology and public
policy. Second and third thoughts took into account the absence
of persuasive supporting data concerning any such ideological
intent of the mass electorate. First tentatively and then with
greater certitude, conventional wisdom shifted.

On the Democratic side the initial reaction had been that a
continued repudiation of the "New Deal"/"New Frontier"/
"Great Society" programs meant (in 1985) that the contest for
the presidency in 1988 must be pursued with centrist candidates
who could not be tarred with the big government, high-
spending brush. Among Republicans, the question seemed to
be largely which wing on the right, the secular or the religious,
would be better suited to continue the sponsorship of programs
that reduce the federal government's presence on the domestic
front while increasing support for a militarily oriented anti-
Communist foreign policy.[1]

Sober reexamination of the many and varied studies of public opinion that followed the 1984 election altered these complementary scenarios. Postelection analyses made clear that
attitudes on spending for defense and domestic social policies
had undergone dramatic reversals during the first four years of
the Reagan presidency. Public exposure to arguments between

the Democrat-controlled House and the Republican Administration over the size of the defense budget led to a clear-cut
plurality of preferences in 1984 for an absolute reduction, not
merely a slowdown, in defense spending. Although sentiment
concerning domestic spending changed less dramatically, there
was also a massive shift away from the earlier demand for
decreases in governmental spending and activity. On virtually
every front having to do with the role of the government in
the affairs of the society, 1984 saw an end to the demand for
more conservative policies and often witnessed substantial support for returning to more spending and greater governmental
activity.[2]

Measuring Change, 1980-84

The data base available for documenting simultaneous conclusions about both party elites and party masses, relevant to
the question of national ideological change, is less substantial
than we might like. As noted earlier, in the attempt to maximize
similarities between mass and elite in the 1984 data collections,
the overlap between the 1980 and 1984 elite collections was
severely truncated. Limiting the analysis to elite changes between 1980 and 1984 and limiting the inspection of change
among party followers to precisely comparable evidence leaves
only the eight specific indicators (see Chapter 1) for both years.
Nevertheless, because the patterns of change exposed by those
eight items fit all that we know more substantially about the
overall patterns of change in the electoral mass, we are confident that we can extend those conclusions to summarize similar patterns of change among the presidential party elites.

The first four years of the Reagan presidency produced a
visible extension of the ideological polarization of the parties
that had taken place during the later 1970s (discussed at length
in *Parties in Transition*). In the first instance there was an
increase in the magnitude of difference separating Democratic
from Republican elites and Democratic from Republican rank

Table 3. Intraparty Changes in Ideology and Policy Preferences, 1980-84

| | Democratic Party | | Republican Party | |
	Elites	Rank & File	Elites	Rank & File
Ideology	+11	+ 6	+ 1	+ 2
Abortion	+19	+11	− 8	− 4
Moral Majority	+ 7	+ 1	+13	− 1
Women's movement	+27	+16	+13	−29
Blacks	+ 1	− 8	−19	0
Busing	+12	− 3	+13	+ 5
Defense	+74	+58	+32	+10
Detente	+25	+ 2	+22	−21

Entries reflect percentage-point changes in group means between 1980 and 1984. A plus (+) indicates a net shift in the liberal direction; a minus (−) reflects a shift in the conservative direction. Wording of items and scoring of responses are described in Appendix B.

and file. This was the result of somewhat different changes that took place within each of these four party groups.

As Table 3 reveals, there was substantial variation, item by item, in the pattern of change among party rank-and-file supporters. Nevertheless, among Republicans there is marginal evidence of a limited overall shift of mass supporters to the right, although changes in the sense of being a liberal or a conservative do not fit the pattern formed by four of the other seven specific items. Among rank-and-file Democrats, four of the eight single-item indicators appear to reflect varying degrees of movement to the left, a movement that permeated all but the racial domain. Although neither set of party supporters appeared to undergo any very dramatic change between the two years, the net result of two minor countervailing movements produced a slight increase in party polarization among the rank-and-file supporters of the two parties.

Within the presidential party elites, the picture of change

among the Republican activists was not as ambiguous as among the Republican rank and file. Although two items suggested a movement to the right, four items indicated even larger movements to the left; and the net result was a clear leftward drift among Republican activists. Their Democratic counterparts moved quite visibly, and somewhat further, in the same direction. With only one exception, the indicators produced marked evidence of increasing support for liberal sentiments among Democratic elite activists.

Because the number of Democratic elites moving to the left so thoroughly outnumbered the leftward drifting Republicans, the net result at the elite level was an increase of interparty differences of about the same magnitude as that witnessed among the rank and file. Contrary to popular wisdom, therefore, it seems fair to characterize aggregate changes in ideological predispositions and policy preferences between 1980 and 1984 as having produced a general movement to the left, accompanied by a small increase in the magnitude of Democratic and Republican differences, among both the party elites and rank-and-file party supporters.

The differences across the various items indicating ideological or issue preferences are highlighted in Table 4. Clearly, attitudes toward the Moral Majority made no contribution to the overall increase in party polarization. Three other items reflect increased polarization on one level but not in the other, but the remaining four items indicate substantial increases in Democratic-Republican differences on both elite and mass levels.

The evidence of increased interparty differences is even more persuasive if we relax our demands for strict comparability across time. The four multi-item measures of generally comparable substantive content in both years show that party differences were accentuated on questions of domestic social issues and foreign and defense policy; party differences were maintained in both elite and mass assessments of traditional partisan group associations; and only in their evaluations of

Table 4. Changes in Interparty Differences, 1980-84

	Elites	Rank & File
Ideological self-designation	+ 10	+ 4
Abortion	+ 27	+ 15
Moral Majority	− 6	+ 2
Women's movement	+ 14	+ 45
Blacks	+ 20	− 8
Busing	+ 9	− 8
Defense	+ 42	+ 48
Detente	+ 3	+ 23
Average	+ 15	+ 15

Entries reflect 1984 increases (+) or decreases (−) in the 1980 differences between Democratic and Republican groups. The scores therefore reflect changes in ideological polarization of the parties between 1980 and 1984.

New Politics groups was there a decrease in party differences between 1980 and 1984.

While differences between parties were accentuated by the politics of the early 1980s, intraparty homogeneity increased within both parties on both mass and elite levels between 1980 and 1984. The increase in intraparty homogeneity and the volatility of the role of party factions in providing structure for differences in ideological predispositions are captured in Table 5.

Taking the individual's ideological designation of self as our illustrative indicator, we found that in 1980 the factional schisms among the elites of both parties were little short of astounding. The supporters of Edward Kennedy formed a small but extreme left wing within the Democratic party, a faction made up almost exclusively of self-declared liberals. Jimmy Carter's support both in 1976 at the time of his nomination and again four years later was, by Democratic elite standards, relatively conservative. Although the Carter supporters in 1980 were predominantly activists who were liberal by their own

Table 5. Intraparty Factionalism Reflected in Mean Scores on Ideological Self-Designation

		Elite Supporters	Rank & File Supporters
		DEMOCRATS	
1980	Kennedy	+81	+15
	Carter	+34	+ 2
Point difference between factions		47	13
1984	Hart	+70	+19
	Mondale	+67	+ 8
Point difference between factions		3	11
Change in factional differences		44-point reduction	2-point reduction
		REPUBLICANS	
1980	Reagan	−94	−43
	Others	−40	−40
Point difference between factions		54	3
1984	Reagan	−93	−43
	Others	−55	−30
Point difference between factions		38	13
Change in factional differences		16-point reduction	10-point increase

Entries indicate plurality of liberals over conservatives (+), or conservatives over liberals (−). The measure of ideological self-designation is described in Appendix B; measures of candidate support in Appendix C.

lights, the gap between the two party wings was reflected in a massive 47-percentage-point difference in the preponderance of liberal over conservative predispositions.

The Republican elite of 1980 were comparably divided, with virtual unanimity among Reagan supporters producing the aura of unalloyed conservatism that characterized his candidacy if not his subsequent presidency. Members of the Republican presidential elite whose first choice for the nomination in 1980 did not include Ronald Reagan were not numerous, but they were at least as different from the Reaganites as the Kennedy supporters were from the Carterites.

In 1980 the elite polarization between intraparty factions as well as between parties was the more notable because of the relative homogeneity of the rank and file in both parties. Although ordinary citizens who preferred Kennedy and Reagan again constituted the polar extremes, they were neither as different from each other nor as different from the other factions of their respective parties as was the case at the elite level.

By 1984 the gap between leadership factions had narrowed on both sides. As a clear testimony to Reagan's leadership, the loyal opposition of those members of the Republican elite who did not prefer his candidacy had moved visibly to the right and had reduced the interfactional gap by approximately 16 percentage points. Equally significant as an influence on national presidential politics in the 1980s was the fact that the Reagan enthusiasts among the Republican elite were persistently monolithic in their self-declared conservatism in both 1980 and 1984. This single-item indicator of change within the Republican party elite suggests a movement to the right that runs counter to much other evidence suggesting a modest drift in the liberal direction. Given the multiplicity of indicators available to us, it seems appropriate at this point to emphasize the evidence of increased party homogeneity on the single measure that is most comparable for 1980 and 1984.

The most striking and perhaps the most surprising of the indicators of change among elite factions is the evidence of the closing of the ideological gap in 1984 among Democrats. Gary Hart and Walter Mondale replaced Kennedy and Carter as the principal contenders, and there were certainly those observers who saw Hart as the inheritor of the left-leaning, New Politics contingent that had favored George McGovern, Morris Udall, and Ted Kennedy before him. The supporting evidence, however, is exceedingly thin on this point. Both on the general ideological indicator and on the other measures of policy preferences, the elite activists in the Hart and Mondale camps were scarcely distinguishable from each other. With both candidates markedly more liberal than the dominant Carter faction of four years earlier, the data reinforced our sense of a liberal Democratic leadership that continued to move to the left during the 1980s despite the resounding electoral victory of the conservative Republican incumbent president.

Among the party rank and file there was a more substantial, although still modest, indication that Hart supporters tended to be somewhat more liberal than the Mondale followers. Indeed, within the mass electorate the differences were of about the same magnitude as those separating Kennedy and Carter supporters in 1980. It would be making much ado about very little to argue an increased homogeneity among rank-and-file Democratic partisans; the factional wings remained marginally different from each other and dramatically less "liberal" in their sentiments than their party's activist elite. Nevertheless, if there was even a small reduction in the distance between the contending factions, this stands in at least minor contrast to the increased differentiation within the Republican party. Just as the Reagan elite stood unchanging on the extreme right, so Reagan rank-and-file supporters showed no dilution of their preponderant commitment to the conservative cause. On the other hand, the rank-and-file supporters of more centrist Republican candidates had actually moved a very small distance toward the center. Since the evidence here is limited to a single measure, and the evidence of intraparty changes could have been produced by a shift from conservative to liberal on the part of only 5 percent of those not preferring Reagan, over-interpretation of the data is a clear and present danger. Never-theless, there may be real political significance in the fact that the Republican rank and file at least did not follow their leaders in the minimization of factional differences in the midst of the Reagan presidency.

Just as the party elites provide the dramatic contrasts in interparty ideological polarization, so they provide the more dramatic evidence of intraparty dynamics that produce change in factional alignments. The contrasts as well as the similarities between 1980 and 1984 are evidence that candidacies may both disclose and obscure the factionalism that is ever a part of national politics. At the same time, the two centers of national mass partisan strength stand as more or less pale reflectors of the leadership's opinion, and suggest rather glacierlike move-ment across limited periods of time. Elsewhere we have noted a conclusion to which I shall return: namely, the ideological revolution in American politics during the Reagan era was primarily a revolution at the top of the Republican power pyra-mid that was scarcely a consequence of change in the broad base of partisan support.[3]

The Measurement of Group Differences

Thus far we have approached the topic of similarities and differences among party masses and elites entirely by com-paring and contrasting mean positions of different groups of political actors. The mean is in many ways the most simple and understandable base for comparison, and it is probably the implicit measure used in ordinary political discourse. One can emphasize simplicity, however, only at the cost of ignoring other information that might provide some insight into how similar and how different two groups of political actors are. Every group mean, or average, is a summary of a "distribution" that portrays each individual member's contribution to the group mean. The full distribution reveals whether the mean is also the median—dividing the group into an equal number of people above and below—or the modal value shared by the largest proportion of the group being "measured." The same mean may be produced by a sharply divided group in which large concentrations of members at either extreme largely cancel each other out, or it may characterize a group in which virtually everybody is at or near the average location on the measure. And neither the concentration around the mean nor the polarizations remote from it would be distinguishable from a relatively flat "rectangular" distribution that produced the same average. In comparing elites with rank-and-file voters, we were interested in knowing more than that the various group means were similar or different. Our interest included comparisons of the full distributions.

To capture information about differing distributions beyond the differences of means, we turned to a somewhat more sensitive and complex device—the correlation, a standard statistic for comparing groups. If two groups are identical with regard to means and the other statistical characteristics of an attribute on which they are being compared, the full distributions of the attributes will be very similar, and the differences between them will approach the value of zero. As the groups diverge, the correlation between the distinctions separating the groups (Democrats from Republicans, for example, or elites from masses) and their respective distributions on the attribute being compared (attitudes toward New Politics groups, for example) will increase up to the point where they are completely different. More often, there will be large but less than perfect correlations between being a member of one group (Democratic elite) characterized by a high score on attribute X (liberal predisposition) and being a member of a second group (Republican elite) characterized by a very low score on the same attribute. By the same token, if the groups are not very different, there may be a very low correlation between being a member of one or another elite group (Hart supporters or Mondale supporters)

Table 6. Dissimilarities between Activists and Rank and File,
Measured by Ideological Self-Designations

Democrats		Republicans	
1980		1980	
Overall	.31	Overall	.33
Supporters of Kennedy	.54	Supporters of Reagan	.50
Supporters of Carter	.18	Supporters of others	.04
1984		1984	
Overall	.38	Overall	.36
Supporters of Mondale	.38	Supporters of Reagan	.45
Supporters of Hart	.40	Supporters of others	.07

Entries are correlations between ideological self-designation scores of elites and rank-and-file party followers: the larger the correlation, the greater the differences in the scores.

and having a unique sense of ideological self-designation (liberal, moderate or conservative).

By examining the simple correlations produced by comparing the distributions of two groups, one obtains a somewhat revised sense of the similarities deduced from the preceding table. Table 6 shows that the net result of changes in distributions of ideological self-designation among Republicans between 1980 and 1984 did very little to alter the similarities or differences between Republican leaders and Republican followers. In 1980 the comparison of all Republican elites with the national Republican rank and file produced a measure of dissimilarity—a correlation (r)—of .33, closer to complete similarity (.00) than to maximum difference (1.00) yet distinguishable from identity. Four years later the degree of similarity was virtually the same: .36 instead of .33. Subdividing both elite and mass populations into party factions shows that in 1980 elite Reagan supporters were markedly different from rank-and-file Reagan supporters (r = .50), and four years later there had been only a slight increase in similarity (to r = .45).

By contrast, in both years the elite members of the non-Reagan wing of the party were very similar to the rank-and-file Republicans who shared their relative lack of enthusiasm for Reagan. The change in the elites' mean positions noted in Table 5 did not seriously intrude on this similarity, and four years later the great similarity of the mass and elite groups, reflected in the 1980 correlation of .04, was still present in the correlation of .07.

Changes in the mean positions of Democratic elite groups had been much more dramatic than those on the Republican side and, in turn, produced evidence of greater change in the extent of mass-elite linkage. In no instance among Democrats was there evidence of the close similarity observed between non-Reaganite Republicans. The strongest indicator of mass-elite rapport among Democrats was provided by the relative similarity of ideological predispositions among Carter's supporters when the correlation or dissimilarity score (mass and elite in 1980) was only .18. In that year, just as the relative extremity of the Reagan elite was reflected in a substantial degree of estrangement from his rank and file supporters (r = .50), the elite supporting Kennedy were at least equally different from his mass base of support in the electorate (r = .54).

The closing of the factional gap among the Democratic elite four years later produced two sets of candidate supporters that were very much alike. The respective degrees of similarity with their rank-and-file bases reflected much less rapport than had been enjoyed in the Carter camp four years earlier, although both Hart and Mondale were less distant from their mass bases than the Kennedy elite had been in 1980.

Returning to the topic of intraparty factionalism, with the new measure of group similarities and dissimilarities we can replicate our earlier report of factionalism pertaining to the single indicator of ideological self-designation and then extend the analysis to the other seven single-item measures of policy

Table 7. Changes in Intraparty Factionalism between 1980 and
1984

	Within Democratic Elites	Within Democratic Rank & File	Within Republican Elites	Within Republican Rank & File
Ideological self-designation	−.37	−.03	−.08	+.06
Abortion	.00	+.02	−.05	−.11
Moral Majority	−.05	+.10	−.09	−.12
Women's movement	−.19	+.03	−.17	−.12
Blacks	−.12	−.03	−.07	−.15
Busing	−.13	+.08	−.13	−.03
Defense	−.19	−.02	+.01	+.06
Detente	.00	+.02	−.14	+.07
Average	−.13	+.02	−.09	−.04

Entries are correlations based on differences in correlations between scores for candidate preference groups in 1980 and 1984. Minus (−) indicates a decrease in intraparty differences, therefore an increase in intraparty homogeneity; conversely; plus (+) reflects an increase in intraparty factionalism.

preference common to our 1980 and 1984 investigations. As Table 7 documents, the correlational measure supports our earlier conclusions in all four comparisons of the single measure of liberal-conservative predispositions. Intraparty factionalism declined everywhere except among the Republican masses, where factionalism increased. On the other hand, extending the analysis to include other indicators of policy preference produces a modification of our general description of intraparty change, but largely where the Republican rank and file is concerned.

We earlier noted and can now reaffirm a marked decline in factionalism within the Democratic elite. The increase in party homogeneity was greatest on the measure of liberal-conservative predispositions, but although the magnitude of this change was not matched on any other policy measure, five of the remaining seven individual items also reflected decreased factionalism among Democratic activists. Within the Republican elite, the overall pattern of change was very much like that of the Democrats in all but matters of detail. The overall pattern of reduced factionalism was more uniform among Republicans, and—except for the one item reflecting ideological self-designation—of the same magnitude as for the Democrats.

At the mass level the marginality of the earlier evidence of reduced factionalism among Democrats is reinforced by the overall pattern of marginal changes in varying directions on the other seven indicators of party homogeneity. The overall average suggests a minimal increase in factionalism, largely the consequence of increased disagreement concerning the Moral Majority and busing. However, the prudent conclusion would still seem to emphasize the limited nature of overall changes in the factionalism of rank-and-file Democrats.

Among the Republican masses the extension of our analysis to include other content domains alters the conclusion that Republican supporters defied the general trend toward less intraparty factionalism. The full array of eight measures of factionalism underscores the limitations of any single, simple generalization. Where the new moral issues and the groups relevant to social change were concerned, Republican rank-and-file supporters reflected the more general pattern of decreased intraparty factionalism. At the same time, their attitude toward defense and detente fit the "deviant" pattern of increased factionalism first observed on the measure of liberal-conservative predispositions. The clarity of these latter assessments undercuts any hasty acceptance of an overall "average" figure suggesting a pervasive decrease in factionalism within the Republican masses.

In general, it would seem best to conclude that both sets of party elites experienced a diminution of factionalism between 1980 and 1984, while neither set of rank-and-file supporters

Table 8. Measures of Interparty Polarization

	Elites			Rank & File		
	1980	1984	Change	1980	1984	Change
Ideological self-designation	.72	.76	+04	.34	.37	+03
Pro-life[1]		.43			.11	
Abortion	.28	.42	+14	.01	.06	+05
Moral Majority[1]	.64	.69	+05	.06	.10	+04
Gay rights[1]		.56			.15	
ERA	.68			.17		
Aid to women		.62			.21	
Women's movement[1]	.62	.67	+05	.17	.26	+09
Blacks[1]	.46	.51	+05	.19	.09	−10
Busing	.53	.56	+03	.21	.16	−05
Inflation	.59			.16		
Pollution	.51			.14		
Defense	.53	.72	+19	.19	.28	+09
Detente	.48	.53	+05	.07	.20	+13
Central America		.70			.17	
Average	.55	.60	+05	.16	.18	+02

Entries are correlations (r) between Democratic and Republican scores: the larger the correlation, the greater the difference. Plus (+) indicates increased interparty polarization; minus (−) indicates increased similarity, decreased polarization.

[1]Scores based on "feeling thermometer" ratings; other scores are based on single items; both are described in Appendix B.

revealed a like degree of change either enhancing or minimizing party cohesiveness.

Applying the same correlational measure of group similarities to our analysis of interparty polarization produces a straightforward confirmation of the more limited analysis based on Table 4. Although there are some variations in the magnitude of the different measures, evidence of increased or decreased partisan polarization is matched item for item in Tables 4 and 8. Between 1980 and 1984 there was an increase in interparty differentiation on all eight of the measures of policy-relevant attitudes of party elites and on six of the eight measures of the preferences of party masses.

3

Mass-Elite Similarities

By the midpoint of the Reagan presidency, the polarization of
Democrats and Republicans was sharply evident on all six of
the general multiple-item indicators of policy preferences and
issue positions derived from our 1984 data collection. Differences were, as in 1980, much sharper among elite activists
than among rank-and-file party supporters. And as Tables 9
and 10 indicate, there were substantial variations in the magnitude of interparty differences among the six content domains
that we shall examine throughout this discussion.

Whether the pattern of differences across the six indicators
contains any surprises largely depends on one's expectations.
For instance, in retrospect, it does *not* seem surprising to discover that at both elite and mass levels, partisans are most
sharply differentiated by the traditional associations of economic and ideological group interests that have long distinguished Democrats from Republicans. Our measure, based on
ratings of the traditional groups associated with partisan politics
(Democrats, Republicans, union leaders, business leaders, liberals, and conservatives) reveals almost no overlap in the distributions of Democratic and Republican elite activists, with
respective means of 21 and 89 and a dissimilarity score of .89.
Partisan differences among rank-and-file party supporters are
not quite as sharp, yet there is no question that party identifiers
differ markedly in the appraisal of these groups. The means
for the mass samples of Democrats and Republicans are 37
and 66, respectively, and the dissimilarity score is .63.

Given the attention accorded many of the new political
themes concerned with moral and social issues in the early

Table 9. Distributions and Means of Elite Policy Preferences 1984

	Liberal/ Conservative		Social Issue		Foreign Policy		Domestic Spending		New Politics		Traditional Groups	
	Dem.	Rep.	Dem.	Rep.	Dem.	Rep.	Dem.	Rep.	Dem.	Rep.	Dem.	Rep.
Liberal	11	—	24	1	57	4	7	—	0	0	22	—
	32	—	19	1	16	4	11	1	—	0	14	0
	29	3	9	3	16	11	17	2	31	2	23	0
	21	15	13	15	6	14	18	4	16	4	11	0
							18	10	22	9	11	—
Center	7	34	10	12	4	23	14	13	12	12	6	2
			1	28			7	19	10	3	3	3
	2	38	2	27	1	16	4	18	5	21	2	5
							2	14	4	27	1	8
							1	8	1	21	1	17
										4		22
Conservative	—	9	—	5	1	28	1	9	—	1	—	43
Mean	32	72	27	70	15	67	29	56	39	64	21	89
Number of cases	996	906	585	469	1047	946	1013	912	964	862	946	884

See Appendix B for descriptions of the measures. Means are based on a standard transformation of all measures to a scale ranging from 0 (liberal) to 100 (conservative). Appendix B describes each transformation.

Table 10. Distributions and Means of Mass Policy Preferences 1984

	Liberal/ Conservative		Social Issue		Foreign Policy		Domestic Spending		New Politics		Traditional Groups	
	Dem.	Rep.	Dem.	Rep.	Dem.	Rep.	Dem.	Rep.	Dem.	Rep.	Dem.	Rep.
Liberal	3	—	2	—	16	4	6	1	0	0	5	0
					—	15	1	0	0	5	0	—
	12	3	4	1	12	7	20	12	15	8	12	—
			5	9			20	12	16	12	12	1
	13	3	16	9	23	15	18	20	22	20	19	4
											15	8
Center	58	42	21	19	25	25	13	24	17	15	19	19
											7	13
	9	23	21	25	15	25	3	9	15	21	4	17
			20	25			2	6	7	14	2	12
	6	24	6	15	7	14	1	2	4	7	1	13
							—	1	2	2	—	6
Conservative	1	3	1	4	3	10	—	—	3	2	—	8
Mean	46	61	54	64	40	57	25	34	46	52	37	66
Number of cases	1063	877	424	378	1060	871	543	502	771	688	777	703

See Appendix B for descriptions of measures and scores underlying the computation of means.

1980s, it may come as a surprise to note that among our six indices, partisan differentiation is least pronounced on the measure assessing positive and negative attitudes toward New Politics groups (including women's liberation, gay rights, Moral Majority, and pro-choice groups). Both the differences of party means and the correlation measures of party dissimilarity reveal relatively limited interparty differences in this domain. The policy questions providing a direct reflection of attitudes on the new social issues produce somewhat greater differentiation between Democrats and Republicans, but—particularly among the mass supporters—the differences are minute when compared to the clear agreement to disagree in assessments of traditional partisan associations.

A second contrast with the political rhetoric of the 1980s is the surprising lack of party differentiation on questions concerning preferences for change in the level of governmental expenditure for domestic programs. The indicator of attitudes toward financial support for domestic programs proved to be unique among the indicators in many of our subsequent analyses. Mass partisans differed less in their attitudes toward spending than in any other of the six domains except regard for New Politics groups. It is also of interest to note a deviation from the usual pattern of elite activists being more extreme than rank-and-file partisans. The very considerable support for domestic spending that can be noted among Democratic elites was exceeded slightly by support, or demand, for increased expenditures on the part of the Democratic rank and file. The topic of domestic spending was also the only one of the six in which the Republican rank and file actually joined Democrats, elite and mass, in a predominantly liberal preference for increased expenditures.

As a final note of discontinuity with public rhetoric on this topic, it can be seen that Republican elite activists were almost evenly divided on the question of spending, with only a modest plurality favoring reductions rather than increases. All told, because of the strong support for increased spending among

Table 11. Mean Scores for Policy Preferences, 1984

Policy Domain	Elite		Mass	
	Dem.	Rep.	Dem.	Rep.
Liberal/				
conservative	32*	72	46	61
Social issues	27	70	54	64
Foreign	15	67	40	57
Spending	29	56	25	34
New Politics	39	64	46	52
Traditional				
groups	21	89	37	66

The entries are taken from Tables 9 and 10.

rank-and-file Democrats and in the absence of Republican preferences in step with the Reagan anti-spending rhetoric, attitudes
toward spending join attitudes toward groups associated with
New Politics *and* toward social issues in reflecting minimal
differences between rank-and-file partisans. Other relationships between masses and elite groups are somewhat more
complex.

The general pattern of sharp interparty differences accompanied by clear-cut intraparty differences between masses and
elites reappears when we examine mean scores, or our correlational assessments of dissimilarities, associated with our
indicators of liberal or conservative self-designation and attitudes toward foreign policy. Both indicators join attitudes toward traditional political groups in creating a picture of national
partisan politics that is sharply polarized, at both elite and mass
levels, over questions of basic political philosophy.

The similarities and differences in partisan polarization
among both activists and rank-and-file supporters are conveyed
in Table 11. There, one can also see at a glance the varying
magnitudes of interparty differences associated with each of
our six substantive domains. That information is further sum-

Table 12. Interparty Differences in Policy Preferences, 1984

	Differences of Means		Correlations	
Policy Domain	Elite	Mass	Elite	Mass
Liberal/ conservative	40	15	.76	.37
Social issues	43	10	.69	.26
Foreign policy	52	17	.72	.31
Domestic spending	27	9	.61	.29
New Politics groups	25	6	.58	.15
Traditional groups	68	29	.89	.63

Means entries show the difference between columns 1 and 2, Table 11, for elites; columns 3 and 4, Table 11, for mass supporters. Correlations for the liberal/conservative measure are also found in the top row of Table 8. All measures reflect Democrat-Republican differences.

marized and presented with a combination of data depicting mean differences and correlations reflecting dissimilarity in Table 12. The first two columns of the table reflect the arithmetic summaries of intraparty differences in elite and mass means presented in Table 11. The third and fourth columns present the assessment of differences as correlational measurements of dissimilarity. Although in general the same major message of relative ideological polarization within a content domain is conveyed by both measures, some notable exceptions bear subsequent comment.

The Analytic Paradigm

The ultimate objective of our comparisons of elite activists and mass partisans is to enable us to explore a variety of mass-

elite similarities and dissimilarities. The first dramatic juxtaposition of such comparisons was produced by Herbert
McClosky and his colleagues when they noted that in the
mid-1950s the leaders of the Republican party (represented by
convention delegates to the 1956 convention) had become so
divergent from mass opinion as to leave the Democratic elite
closer than the Republican elite to Republican mass partisans.[1]
Given the expectation that leaders and followers from a single
party should resemble each other more than should leaders from
one party and the followers from another, what McClosky
found was appropriately taken to be an important commentary
on the ideological structure of partisan politics in the immediate
postwar era. Two decades later Kirkpatrick replicated the
McClosky analysis and discovered that with the onset of party
reform, largely within the Democratic party, it was by then
the Democratic leadership that had so estranged itself from
mass opinion as to leave the opposition elite better matched
with its own Democratic followers (as well as with the Republicans' own rank and file).[2] The extent to which the dissimilarity between Democratic activists and Democratic
supporters dramatized the consequences of institutional reforms in the Democratic party provided the foundation for the
Kirkpatrick thesis of the emergence of a "new presidential
elite."

In a sequel to the argument that a new set of ultraliberal,
issue-oriented amateurs had replaced centrist party profession-
als in dominating the Democratic party, the Miller-Jennings
analysis argued that, eight years later, symmetry had been
restored to the two-party system as Republican estrangement
came to equal that of the Democrats. Although our data did
not support the thesis of a return to the circumstances of 1956,
we did argue that the extremism of a very homogeneous ideological Republican elite had produced a situation in which
Democratic leaders were virtually as close to the Republican
rank and file as were the Republican leaders.[3] We also suggested that the stage may have been set for some further shift

Table 13. Correlational Measures of Elite-Mass Dissimilarity, 1984

Policy Domain	Dem. Elite– Dem. Mass	Dem. Elite– Rep. Mass	Rep. Elite– Dem. Mass	Rep. Elite– Rep. Mass
Liberal/ conservative	+.34	+.60	−.60	−.30
Social issues	+.50	+.64	−.36	−.13
Foreign policy	+.46	+.66	−.44	−.19
Democratic spending	−.11	+.15	−.66	−.52
New Politics	+.18	+.32	−.45	−.33
Traditional	+.37	+.76	−.85	−.57

Entries are correlations (r) between group differences (mass-elite) and the preference distributions of the groups. Signs indicate whether the elite group is more liberal than the mass (+) or more conservative than the mass (−).

in party and policy preferences, which might well punish the Republican extremists as their Democratic counterparts had been punished before them. The election of 1984 proved otherwise. Just as the centrism of Carter provided little electoral protection against the extreme conservative appeal of Reagan in 1980, so the estrangement of Republican leadership in 1984 seemed to carry few electoral consequences in the contest with the centrist Mondale.

It is now clear that whatever else the changes in ideological patterning of party differences produced between 1980 and 1984, they introduced an element of balance in the juxtaposition of the partisan elites with their followers in the partisan rank and file. In Table 13, which compares the similarity of the preferences of the Democratic elites and of the Republican elites with those of the two partisan masses in six different domains, a neat picture of symmetry and balance appears in the substantive domain of ideological predispositions. The Democratic elites were almost exactly as much more like their Democratic followers as the Republican elites were more like *their* followers, and there is no apparent difference in the extent to which Democratic activists resembled Republican masses and Republican activists resembled Democratic masses. In contrast to the sharp interparty differences noted earlier, the dissimilarity scores on ideological location suggest a modicum of absolute agreement between leaders and followers in both parties.

This is quite different from the situation revealed by the five other indicators of policy preferences. On questions of social issues and foreign policy, Republican activists were much closer to their rank-and-file supporters than Democrats were to theirs. And, as seemed to be more generally true of the juxtapositions of followers and leaders in 1972, Republican elites were clearly more like Democratic rank and file on social issues than were the Democratic elites, and they were virtually tied with the Democratic elites in reflecting Democratic mass sentiments in foreign policy.

Something close to a mirror image of these mass-elite linkages characterized attitudes toward spending and New Politics groups. The configuration is particularly striking on the Reagan administration's policy of reducing government spending for domestic programs. The preferences of the Democratic elites were remarkably similar to those of the Republican rank and file, as well as to the Democratic mass-support group. And the estrangement of the Republican leadership from national public opinion on this issue put them at a very considerable distance from their mass supporters as well as from ordinary Democratic partisans.

Circumstances were less extreme where evaluations of New Politics groups were concerned, but there, too, the Democratic leaders equaled the Republican elite in matching Republican rank-and-file sentiments, while their attitudes were an even closer match with those of their Democratic followers. As has been implicit in most such comparisons, this pattern suggests a political advantage for the Democratic elite where assessments of New Politics groups are concerned. This contrasts with the implications of a similar advantage for the Republican elite in the social-issue domain, even though the individual issues are political "causes" for four of the five groups included in the New Politics measure. The differences in the patterns associated with the two New Politics measures strike us as an instance of the more general tension between "symbolic politics" and "real" politics. In an era in which political protest has been accepted as legitimate on both the left and the right, the symbolic politics of representing group interests may produce quite different responses than do disagreements over the specific public policy issues involved. In this example, Republican leadership has the advantage where the argument is over public policy alternatives, but Democratic leadership has the advantage if the contest is defined in terms of symbolic group politics.

Finally, it is interesting to note that despite the parties' agreement to disagree in their assessments of traditional partisan groups, the spread between elite and mass mean scores in both parties indicated a very real limit on intraparty rapport between leaders and followers. Among Republicans the dissimilarities of opinion between masses and elites were particularly notable.

On foreign policy matters, Republican leadership virtually matched Democratic leadership in its similarity to the opinions of the Democratic mass. This pattern was balanced, in turn, where sentiments with regard to New Politics actors were concerned. Here Democratic leadership resembled Republican rank and file as much as did Republican leadership. The relative similarity of the juxtaposition of liberal and conservative predispositions was roughly replicated in assessments of traditional political groups: once more, party leaders were more like their own followers than like those of the opposition; and by and large, although the Democratic elite may have had a small edge, neither party leadership was remarkably closer to the opposition's rank and file.

From this picture it is impossible to conclude as a general matter that in 1984 the leadership of either party demonstrated greater rapport with national public opinion. Although domestic spending and domestic social issues were nearly tied as the least polarized of the issue domains, they represented sharp contrasts in the extent to which there was interparty elite competition for the same set of rank-and-file citizens. On social issues, Republican leaders edged out Democratic leaders in reflecting Democratic rank-and-file sentiments; on spending, Democratic leadership had an even larger edge over Republican leadership in representing the views of the Republican rank and file. The apparently straightforward rank-ordering of partisan groups (from Republican elite through to Democratic elite) was replaced by a much more complex picture of similarities and differences when we moved from the simple juxtapositions of means to the more comprehensive correlational assessments of group similarities and differences.

Interyear Comparisons

A detailed comparison of the data from 1984 with measures generated four years earlier discloses rather remarkable similarities that are important on both substantive and methodological grounds. Despite the limited number of identical items used in studying both masses and elites in both years, there were multi-item measurements with high similarity across the years. Thus, the 1980 study, like the 1984 data collection, produced a multi-item measure of attitudes toward new social issues, a measure of sentiments on foreign policy, a single-item liberal/conservative measure, and measures of attitudes toward New Politics groups and traditional groups. These were all similar to the 1984 measures in the same domains, though by no means identical. To the extent that they *are* functional equivalents of each other, the several pairs of measures permit some interesting cross-year comparisons.

Table 14 displays the means for party masses and party elites for five indexes in both years. The data are notable primarily

Table 14. Comparison of Mean Policy Preference Scores

Policy Domain	Elites		Masses	
	Dem.	Rep.	Dem.	Rep.
Liberal/ conservative				
1984	32	72	46	61
1980	34	64	48	62
Social issues				
1984	27	70	54	64
1980	35	69	49	54
Foreign policy				
1984	15	67	40	57
1980	38	77	59	68
New Politics				
1984	39	64	46	52
1980	18	59	32	43
Traditional groups				
1984	21	89	37	66
1980	23	89	42	67

Entries are means calculated for indexes standardized to range from 0 (liberal) to 100 (conservative); see Appendix B.

for their indication of relative attitudinal stability among both masses and elites of both parties. The 1980 differences across the five domains are almost perfectly preserved in 1984, as are the general magnitudes of both interparty and intraparty mass-elite differences. At the same time, these data support the thesis of modestly increased interparty differences—particularly among the party elites—on the liberal/conservative measures, on social issues, and on foreign policy. They indicate minimal change in assessments of traditional partisan groups, and they show reduced interparty polarization concerning New Politics.

The interyear comparisons confirm the leftward drift for the Democratic elite, but they suggest interdomain variations in the change of the other three groups.

The general persistence of the attitudinal patterns is the more remarkable because the 1984 study constitutes a totally independent replication of 1980. For the national mass samples, completely different respondents were selected from two entirely different sampling frames, one created for the 1978 National Election Studies and the second drawn in 1982 following the 1980 census. The noted lack of precise identity in items that make up the various indexes contributes to the separateness and independence of the two pairs of data collections. The 1980 population of elites did contain some persons who would repeat as delegates in 1984, and some 1980 delegates were active in both years (although not as delegates in 1984); nevertheless, the 1980 elites were largely a different group from the 1984 elites, who were chiefly delegates from that year. Except for this overlapping of the membership in the two elites, the two sets of data used in this book set the foundation for a textbook example of analytic replication. We began analysis with the assurance that whatever differences we observed between 1980 and 1984, they were not the consequence of distributional differences imposed by the independence of our statistical bases. And we can conclude with the assurance that virtually all our conclusions (except those pertaining to interyear comparisons) are supported by a precise and detailed replication of evidentiary tests in 1980.

The contribution of the circulation of elites to linkage between elite and mass candidate preference groups is reviewed briefly in Table 15. We sorted out three categories from our universe of sometime delegates: those who were mobilized in 1984 after having been inactive in the 1980 presidential campaign; those who dropped out of the presidential politics in 1984 after having been active delegates in 1980; and those who were active in both years (differentiated by the three patterns

Table 15. Circulation of Elites and Changes in Mass-Elite Similarities

Activity Pattern		Democrats			Republicans		
1980	1984	Mondale	Hart	Total	Reagan	Other	Total
Disengaged							
delegate	Inactive nondelegate	.13	.06	.10	.12	.04	.06
Continually active							
delegate	nondelegate but active	.33	.33	.33	.41	.02	.33
delegate	delegate	.25	.16	.58	.36	.02	.30
nondelegate but active	delegate	.37	.37	.40	.42	.10	.37
Mobilized							
inactive nondelegate	delegate	.16	.27	.31	.14	.03	.13
Overall similarity:							
1980			.31			.33	
1984			.38			.36	

All entries are correlations between elite and rank-and-file policy preference scores: the larger the correlation, the greater the difference.

of delegate status that are the logical consequence of our classification scheme). Some of the same generalizations observed in the analysis of the 1972-80 elite circulation (reported in *Parties in Transition*) reappear. Somewhat paradoxically, in both the earlier analysis (summarized in Table 2, Chapter 1) and the present inquiry (reported in Table 15), the continually active elites in both parties were *less* like their parties' rank-and-file followers than are either those who were mobilized or those who disengaged. There seems to be real irony in the fact that delegates who dropped out of the role of campaign activist were most "representative" of their party's rank-and-file supporters. This is quite true for the entire set of party activists in both parties in 1980 and substantially true for the subsets who form the candidates' factions in 1984. A second generalization seems to permeate these analyses: those who were newly mobilized were more like the rank-and-file partisans than those who were continually active, but slightly less representative of rank-and-file distributions of sentiment than the disengaged whom they replaced. Replenishment of the ranks apparently helps maintain rapport with the masses, even though in the short run it may not offset the relative estrangement of the continually active elite participants.

Despite the similarities in the patterns of mass-elite relationship in the two analyses, it is appropriate to note that the theme of replication should always be accompanied by attention to possible alternative interpretations. We know too little about the role of leadership as it influences the mobilization and disengagement of elite activists, and too little about the circumstances under which individual change and compositional change of elites develop, to be confident that sheer replication warrants an immediate conclusion. To put it another way, the sharp differences in the nature of the nominations of Carter, Mondale, and Reagan must have had different consequences for their supporting elites, but the replication of results has so far obscured our vision of what those consequences must have been. While we can proceed with confidence that partisanship and political leadership play major roles in shaping mass-elite linkages, the contribution of the circulation of the campaign elites must remain a matter of at least some uncertainty.

4

Linkage Mechanisms: Party

The importance of party in democratic government is matched only by the multitude of forms in which party appears. The one-time classic formulation of party as an entity embodied in the mind of the elector, in the campaign organization, or in the organizing structure of government has been outmoded as it becomes more and more apparent that the manifestations of party are almost infinitely varied both in form and in substance. This became more obvious as we tried to locate empirical evidence for the theoretical origins and consequences of the various concerns about party that were involved in this study treating presidential delegate campaign activists as party elites.

We pursued the analogue to party identification in the electorate by asking our elite activists to specify the strength of the enthusiasm with which they supported their parties: "Please choose the number [from 1 to 7] that best describes how strongly you support your political party." Although only small minorities offered more than minor qualifications to their self-portrayal as strong party supporters, those minorities add to our understanding of how party structures ideology among the political elite.

Our concern for the organizational manifestation of party was reflected in a question asking the delegates to describe the strength of the party organization back home: "Is the party organization in your local community very strong, fairly strong, not very strong, or not strong at all?" This question provoked something like a 60-40 split between delegates from strong organizational settings and those from weak organizational contexts.

As an analogue to the traditional assessment of the importance of party in government, we asked the delegates to indicate the relative importance of party as a guide to their convention hall decisions.

As an extension of our interest in establishing the importance that campaign activists attached to the political party, we asked for the extent to which the support of party motivated their campaign activities.

In yet another context we probed for information about the assistance provided by party in helping the would-be delegate achieve delegate status.

In most of these contexts it is less than totally clear what the delegates understood the referent of "party" to be. Thus, being helped by the party as one worked to become a delegate may have meant formal support by a party organization, sponsorship by party leaders, or some other more amorphous sense in which "party" provided help to one's candidacy. Even if party was specified as the focus of campaign activity, it is not clear whether the meaning was support of party leadership, support of party principles, or support of party in order to be on the winning side in the election.

What we have learned about party as a link between leaders and followers rests on delegates' reported images of party. Fortunately, it appears that commonalities in their associations with party, and in their contrasts between party and other political referents, strongly imply a shared political culture in which party has common meanings across partisan boundaries and in many different decision-making contexts. Nevertheless, one of the by-products of our attempt to understand more fully the contribution of party to mass-elite linkages has been to learn, in turn, more about the variety of ways in which the nature of party is made manifest in the course of the presidential selection process. Some of these ways will become apparent as we proceed with our task of specifying the circumstances or conditions under which there is greater or lesser similarity in the policy-related attitudes of political activists and their fellow partisans in the mass electorate.

Elite Party Support

An examination of variations in linkage associated with differing degrees of intensity or strength of party identification among elite activists immediately encounters what appears to be a substantial paradox concerning the central role of party as a mechanism for linking mass and elite sentiments. Comparing strong party supporters and weak party supporters provides pervasive evidence, for both parties, that a stronger sense of party support *limits* the extent to which elites resemble masses. The evidence is virtually unbroken, whether one compares national means, mean differences of state level means, or correlational indicators.

This is not to say there are not variations across our six indicators. As Table 16 shows, the evidence that weak partisans among the activists are more likely to resemble fellow partisans in the electorate at large is ambiguous in our assessments of 1984 Democratic attitudes toward domestic spending.[1] And the findings are virtually null in 1980 for Republicans on ideology and in 1984 for the Democrats with regard to social issues. At the other extreme, the contrast between strong and weak party supporters among the activists is clear in the assessments of the traditional partisan groups, and scarcely less evident in the other three indicators—liberal/conservative ideology, foreign policy, and assessments of New Politics groups. In five domains, strong party supporters in both parties were consistently *less* likely to resemble party rank-and-file followers than were weak party supporters. This suggests, of course, that despite the stark differences between the parties portrayed in Chapter 2, strength of party identification somehow tends to blur the same differences.

This conclusion is sharply and unequivocally supported on the Republican side of the aisle. It may be that our line of demarcation between "strong" and "weak" supporters is responsible for the party differences; our cutoff point left a smaller, possibly more unique, set of Republican activists separated from their peers than was true on the Democratic side

Table 16. Elite Party Support and Similarity of Mass and Elite Attitudes

Strength of Elite Party Support	Liberal/Conservative		Social Issue		Foreign Policy		Domestic Spending		New Politics		Traditional Groups	
	Dem.	Rep.	Dem.	Rep.	Dem.	Rep.	Dem.	Rep.	Dem.	Rep.	Dem.	Rep.
1980												
Strong	.38	.07	.31	.36	.36	.19			.33	.30	.51	.61
Weak	.29	.04	.21	.22	.25	.07			.20	.18	.24	.36
Difference	−.09	−.03	−.10	−.14	−.14	−.12			−.13	−.12	−.27	−.25
1984												
Strong	.38	.35	.50	.15	.47	.23	.09	.54	.21	.35	.45	.62
Weak	.22	.06	.48	.02	.33	.02	.18	.49	.09	.17	.16	.28
Difference	−.16	−.29	−.02	−.13	−.14	−.21	+.09	−.05	−.12	−.18	−.29	−.34

All entries in rows 1, 2, 4, and 5 are correlations between policy preference scores of party elites and party rank and file: the larger the correlation, the greater the elite-mass difference. See Appendix C for the measure of party support. The arithmetic differences between similarity measures associated with strong and weak party support are scored to reflect the *decrease* in similarity associated with *strong* party support.

Table 17. Strength of Elite Party Support

	1980		1984	
	Dem.	Rep.	Dem.	Rep.
Strong	70%	83%	73%	83%
Weak	30	17	27	17
	100%	100%	100%	100%
Number of cases	828	520	1063	964

See Appendix C for description of the measure of strength of party support.

(see Table 17). In any event, both in 1980 and 1984, Republican elites who saw themselves as strong party supporters were, on the average, more different—state by state—from their partisan supporters and much more different as a group from their national rank and file than were weak identifiers. The suggestion of a national Republican party orthodoxy in the 1980s is reinforced by our data, and the implications are extended with the evidence of large gaps between the preferences and aspirations of the Republican rank and file and the preferences and commitments of this portion of their party's elite.

The Republican circumstance concerning the strength of party loyalty is the more noteworthy because of the contrast it offers to intraparty *factional* differences that I discuss at length later on. As a preview, note that there are pervasive differences to be observed between the pro-Reagan activists and the "other" group of the Republican elite in both 1980 and 1984. However that may be, Republicans even more than Democrats document the conclusion that although parties provide the dominant structure for ideological and public policy preferences of both masses and elites engaged in American politics, a strong sense of party support on the part of elite activists may actually be dysfunctional for linking mass and elite issue preferences.

Table 18. Strength of Party Support and Mean Scores of Elites

Strength of Elite Party Support	Liberal Conservative		Social Issue		Foreign Policy		Domestic Spending		New Politics		Traditional Groups	
	Dem.	Rep.	Dem.	Rep.	Dem.	Rep.	Dem.	Rep.	Dem.	Rep.	Dem.	Rep.
1980												
Strong	33	65	33	69	37	78			16	60	20	91
Weak	34	60	38	64	40	73			23	55	32	83
Differences	−1	−5	−5	−5	−3	−5			−7	−5	−12	−8
1984												
Strong	31	74	27	70	14	70	28	56	38	65	19	90
Weak	36	64	27	66	18	56	31	56	42	60	29	80
Differences	−5	−10	0	−4	−4	−14	−3	0	−4	−5	−10	−10

Scores range from 0 (most liberal) to 100 (most conservative). Differences indicate the extent to which the scores Strong Supporters' among the elites are *less* like those of the relatively centrist masses; therefore, the signs have the same meaning as in Table 16.

The crucial insight into the nature of the paradox is provided by an examination of average or mean scores on our measures of policy preferences of the elites. First of all, quite predictably, the modal self-characterization of our delegates identified them as, by and large, strong party supporters. As Table 17 indicates, on a scale ranging from 1 (weakest) to 7 (strongest), three out of four Democratic activists and slightly more than four out of five Republicans placed themselves at 6 or 7 on the scale. For 1984 we are thus comparing 780 Democratic activists and 800 Republican activists who describe themselves as strong party supporters with 285 Democrats and 160 Republicans who are simply less strong, in varying degrees, in their support of party.

With the possible exception of two deviations in 1984—among Democrats on social issues and Republicans on domestic spending, where there were only very small differences in the mean scores of stronger and weaker supporters—*weak supporters in both parties were uniformly less extreme in their mean positions on all measures of policy preference.* Thus, strong Democrats were the most liberal, and strong Republicans the most conservative; with weak Democrats and weak Republicans being slightly more moderate than their peers. For instance, Table 18 shows that the 1980 scores on attitudes toward traditional partisan groups ran from a very liberal 20 for strong Democrats to a more conservative 32 for weaker Democrats, and from 83 for weak Republicans to a very conservative 91 for strong Republicans. Given the ubiquitous nature of this pattern, the explication of the "paradox" follows: the intraparty comparisons of elites with masses are comparisons between more extreme elites and more moderate elites, each with a still more moderately positioned party mass. A weaker subjective sense of support for party elites is characteristically associated not with ideological extremism but with moderation. Deviation of weak elite party supporters from the statistical mean of fellow elite partisans is therefore usually in the direction of the mean position of party followers in the mass electorate, producing the greater similarity between mass sentiments and those of weak party supporters within the elite.

Descriptively, the lack of congruence of strongly partisan elites with mass sentiment is not a matter of strong party supporters deviating from a centrist mode to adopt extreme ideological positions that estrange them from party rank and file. The situation is properly seen, rather, as one in which weak party supporters deviate from "extreme" party modes by being *less* extreme in their ideological persuasion, not more extreme, and therefore being *more* like rank-and-file party supporters, not less like them. Even though party differences provide the basic structure for ideological differentiation within the electorate, stronger partisanship on the part of elites separates them from the modal position of the rank-and-file followers. Activists who are weak partisans are more similar to their partisan masses.

It is not uncommon to have American political parties depicted as less ideologically polarized than their European bloc counterparts. Indeed, American politics is frequently characterized as essentially centrist politics. It is now clear that even though this may be true in a comparative sense, within the context of the American political system the elite of the two parties are sharply differentiated and, in comparison with rank-and-file supporters, the partisan elites can fairly be described as ideologically polarized. As a consequence, *any* factor producing elite subgroups that are *less* extreme than the modal positions for party elites in general will generally produce subgroups that are more similar to the centrist masses with whom they are associated.

Party As a Guide to Action

A more easily anticipated contribution of party to mass-elite linkage is its role as the focal point for guiding or organizing the sentiments of those participating in nominating conventions. As one part of our interest in the recruitment and mobilization of political activists, we asked elites to describe the

Table 19. Groups That Helped Delegates

	1980		1984	
	Dem.	Rep.	Dem.	Rep.
Political party	32%	41%	25%	59%
Presidential candidate	18	40	30	16
The voters	30	11	17	10
Social issues groups	5	1	4	1
Traditional groups	16	7	24	14
	100%	100%	100%	100%
Number of cases	408	262	569	458

"Other" responses and "not ascertained" are omitted from tables. See Appendix C for a description of the measure.

sources of assistance to them as they were seeking to become delegates. Party differences in the volunteered attribution of sponsorship as depicted in Table 19 were clear and seemed to fit both party circumstances and subsequent political commentary.

In 1980, with competition for the nomination largely confined to Republicans, Democratic delegates most often reported that they were aided by party or by voters. Republican delegates were twice as likely to recall assistance from contending candidates, although they also reported a high incidence of aid from the party. Four years later the circumstances were reversed: candidate sponsorship was a weak second among Republicans but dominant among Democrats.

Subsequently, we pursued our interest in the role of the sponsors of delegates to inquire about which, if any, of the major recruiting agencies were also the focus of delegate attempts to represent others' points of view during the course of decision-making in the convention. We pursued this line of inquiry in an attempt to recapture the evolving experience of being a delegate, but with no particular interest in accounting for the outcome of any convention decision beyond that of the nomination itself. Given the extent to which delegates were "bound" in their pledged support of candidates for nomination, the referent for our query about representing other points of view was most likely concerned with the various procedural or rulemaking activities of the convention. And to the extent that the information about sponsorship—or representation— was not focused on decisions with explicit policy implications, our questioning apparently tapped some very persuasive orientations that guide elite participation. This follows because differences in attributed representational salience of the various political phenomena were associated with ubiquitous differences in mass-elite similarities for both Republican and Democrats, in both 1980 and 1984.

The two questions of delegate sponsorship and delegate representation predictable drew highly correlated responses; however, systematic differences appeared in both parties. Among both Democratic and Republican elites, but particularly among Democrats, the question of the focus of *representation* identified larger proportions of those who saw themselves as representing candidates than of those who reported having been assisted by a candidate in their efforts to become delegates. The extent to which candidates dominate presidential politics is thus emphasized by the increase in the salience of candidacies in both parties in both years—even after aspiring activists have become delegates, often with help from some source other than a candidate.

Among Democrats, from a fourth to a third of those who reported that they were sponsored by the party subsequently came to represent a particular candidate in the course of the convention. In similar fashion, substantial numbers who entered the lists on behalf of traditional issue interests later saw themselves as representing a candidate in convention deliberations. And comparable fractions of those who described their entry into delegateship as being supported by "the voters" subsequently moved to represent a candidate. Similar changes among Republicans produced somewhat similar variations between preconvention sponsorship and representation in con-

Table 20. Groups That Delegates Represented in Convention

	1980		1984	
	Dem.	Rep.	Dem.	Rep.
Political party	43%	29%	17%	47%
Presidential candidate	49	57	55	33
The voters	8	8	7	8
Social issues groups	6	1	6	2
Traditional groups	13	5	15	10
	100%	100%	100%	100%
Number of cases	431	275	594	476

See Appendix C for a description of the measure.

vention proceedings. Table 20 represents the 1980 and 1984 distributions of responses to the query about representation. It shows substantial similarities between the two parties with regard to the incidence of representing voters, new social issues, and more traditional issues. There is, however, a clear differentiation between parties in the extent to which Democrats reflected the preconvention struggle for the 1984 nomination in their continuing commitment to candidates, while the Republicans in the year of Reagan's renomination were much more concerned with representing their image of the Republican party. Four years earlier, with Reagan undertaking the challenge of the Democratic incumbent, it was the Republican delegates who had concentrated on representing candidate interests in the deliberations of the convention.

The correlates of the decisions to represent party rather than candidates, constituents, or issue commitments present unmistakable evidence that party orientations are associated with providing—or at least facilitating—the linkage between partisan leaders and partisan followers. This stands in strong contrast to the role of party as represented by the subjective reports of the strength of activist support for party.

Among the five alternative foci for representation presented

Table 21. Focus of Representational Efforts and Similarities of Mass-Elite Policy Preferences

Group Represented	Liberal/ Conservative		Social Issues		Foreign Policy		Domestic Spending		New Politics		Traditional Groups	
	Dem.	Rep.	Dem.	Rep.	Dem.	Rep.	Dem.	Rep.	Dem.	Rep.	Dem.	Rep.
1980												
Political party	.14	−.04	.09	−.26	.17	−.09			.16	−.21	.28	−.45
Presidential candidate	.36	−.11	.31	−.40	.34	−.21			.36	−.35	.51	−.57
The voters	.14	.00	.12	−.16	.13	−.07			.14	−.14	.25	−.28
Social issues groups	.25	—	.25	—	.25	—			.24	—	.32	—
Traditional groups	.24	.02	.18	−.17	.18	−.12			.23	−.18	.37	−.26
1984												
Political party	.15	−.20	.37	−.06	.22	−.13	−.16	−.47	.08	−.27	.21	−.48
Presidential candidate	.36	−.29	.55	−.23	.43	−.27	−.08	−.54	.24	−.31	.37	−.49
The voters	.07	−.12	.24	−.03	.17	−.05	−.15	−.36	.03	−.11	.06	−.22
Social issues groups	.22	—	.41	—	.24	—	−.01	—	.15	—	.23	—
Traditional groups	.20	−.19	.36	−.15	.26	−.15	.02	−.31	.12	−.12	.32	−.31

Minus (−) sign attached to a correlation shows that the elite group is more conservative than its mass partisans.

in Table 21 (four for Republicans, because too few Republican activists emphasized social issues to provide a reliable estimate of their positions), among elites in both parties, and on virtually all of our indicators of policy preferences, those who saw themselves as representing party interests in convention decisions more closely resembled fellow partisans in the national rank and file than did their numerous colleagues whose commitment focused on candidate representation.

In a rather remarkable validation of delegates' depiction of their own representational roles, there are only five cases in seventy-seven comparisons in which delegates intending to represent the voters were less representative of their rank-and-file partisans than was some other set of elite activists. With only one exception, those representing candidates' interests were less representative of mass sentiments than were the other delegate groups. And between the boundaries set by those representing candidates at one extreme and those directly representing voters at the other, the representatives of party virtually always matched or outdid the representatives of issue groups in providing a match for mass policy preferences. Overall, whether the measure is one of attitudinal means or correlational assessments of similarity, party interests as a focus for convention decision-making were clearly associated with strong mass-elite linkages.

Once again, the issue of governmental spending played a somewhat deviant role in 1984. Among Democrats, representation of party or of voters was *least* effective in identifying delegates who shared mass sentiments concerning domestic spending. The very fact of moderation in policy preferences, which usually produced greater linkage of elites with masses, was once again dysfunctional for representation in a domain in which the mass position was more extreme than the modal elite position. The visibly more liberal protagonists of issues and candidates provided a better match for mass preference on the level of domestic spending than did the more centrist advocates of party and citizen interests. Apart from this deviation,

Table 22. Elites' Motives for Presidential Campaign Activity

Motive for Campaign Work	1980		1984	
	Dem.	Rep.	Dem.	Rep.
To work for party	43%	50%	37%	59%
To work for an issue	13	6	24	5
To help a candidate	44	44	39	36
	100%	100%	100%	100%
Number of cases	313	231	440	357

See Appendix C for a description of the measure.

however, party was apparently a most reliable *institution* in enhancing mass-elite similarities.

In the analysis of still later stages in the presidential selection process, an increasingly familiar set of findings emerges. *Parties in Transition* paid considerable attention to the changing salience of party as the inspiration for campaign activity. As with the structuring of issue preference, noted in the first chapter, it seemed that party, party faction, and the circulation of party elites all contributed to variations in the importance that could be assigned to party in 1980 as an entity involved in the presidential election campaign. And some point was made of the changes between 1972 and 1980 that restored party to a position of preeminence among Democrats while largely preserving its status among Republicans.

The consequences of interyear and interparty changes in the focus of campaign activity in 1980 and 1984 are not radically different from the changes just noted in representational referents for convention decision-making. As Table 22 illustrates, in 1984 Democrats were more likely to emphasize candidates in their campaigning, and Republicans were more likely to reflect the increased salience of party. However, the relative salience of issues changed more in the context of election campaigning than in the earlier, decision-making phase of the process. While Republicans did narrow the gap between their limited *representational* interests in issues as against the greater Democratic emphasis in 1980 (with a Republican doubling of the proportion that represented issue interests by the 1984 convention [see Table 20]), they did not change the incidence of their concern for issues in the campaign activities of the two convention years. Democrats, on the other hand, showed about the same level of effort to represent issue interests in the convention of 1984 as in the convention of 1980, but they were twice as likely in 1984 as in 1980 to report that they campaigned on behalf of particular issue or policy commitments.

Issues were salient for the efforts of twice as many Democrats as Republicans in the campaign of 1980 (13 percent against 6 percent). The ratio had increased to 5 to 1 by 1984: 24 percent of Democrats and only 5 percent of Republicans reported that they campaigned primarily because they "wanted to work for an issue or for some specific group" (other than party or candidate). It is of more than passing interest to note in Table 22 the extent to which Democratic activists quite apparently reacted and responded to the ideological innovations of the Reagan administration's first four years with a substantial increase in their own preoccupation with issues. It may be of equal interest, although of less obvious consequence, to note how seldom Republicans characterized their efforts to reelect Reagan in 1984 as a commitment to any of the issue groups associated with the New Right in Republican party politics. In any event, our understanding of the meaning and role of party in the creation of mass-elite issue preference linkages is furthered largely by the presence of Democrats concerned with issues as a focus for campaign activity.

Given the importance of party and party faction in the structuring of policy preferences within the national political elite, it is more than simply "interesting" to observe that elite preoccupations with issues provide the most striking foil against which to emphasize just how important party is in the linking

Table 23. Motives for Campaigning and Similarities of Mass-Elite Policy Preferences

Motive	Liberal Conservative		Social Issues		Foreign Policy		Domestic Spending		New Politics		Traditional Groups	
	Dem.	Rep.	Dem.	Rep.	Dem.	Rep.	Dem.	Rep.	Dem.	Rep.	Dem.	Rep.
1980												
Party	.19	.00	.12	−.27	.21	−.10			.32	−.36	.46	−.62
Issue	.28	—	.21	—	.24	—			.27	—	.41	—
Candidate	.28	−.07	.23	−.34	.24	−.20			.15	−.19	.21	−.28
1984												
Party	.14	−.14	.36	−.06	.25	−.08	−.16	−.47	.03	−.22	.24	−.40
Issue	.33	—	.44	—	.32	—	−.02	—	.18	—	.29	—
Candidate	.21	−.23	.37	−.13	.31	−.21	−.14	−.52	.11	−.29	.21	−.44

Minus (−) sign indicates instances in which elites are more conservative than masses.

of mass and elite concerns about ideology, policy, and issues. First, however, a close scrutiny of the data in Table 23 reveals that in 14 of 22 comparisons of mass-elite similarities, delegates who campaigned because they were committed to "party work" were quite clearly more like their rank-and-file counterparts than were delegates who "wanted to help a particular candidate." Four of the other eight comparisons, all in 1984, revealed very small differences. The assessments of New Politics and traditional groups in 1980 produced all four instances in which candidate support clearly exceeded party in enhancing mass-elite similarities. The bulk of the evidence most directly concerning issue preferences (liberalism/conservatism, social issues, and foreign policy) thus supports the conclusion that campaigners preoccupied with party more closely resembled rank-and-file partisans' preferences on issues and ideology than did campaigning elites preoccupied with their favorite candidates.

Only Democrats had enough interest in issues as the focus for campaign activities to give us possibly reliable estimates of mass-elite similarities associated with issue-oriented campaigning. Of the hundreds of elite activists in our sample, only 14 Republicans in 1980 and 19 Republicans in 1984 reported campaigning primarily on behalf of an issue or a nonparty, noncandidate group. Among Democrats, the raw numbers in our study were 42 issue-oriented campaigners in 1980 and 104 in 1984. In 1984 only the spending issue deviated (again) from the ten other comparisons of mass-elite similarities. Domestic spending provided the only setting in which the issue-oriented Democrats were more similar to rank-and-file partisans than was true for party- *or* candidate-oriented campaigners. In 1980 there were no instances in which the issue-oriented were actually *less* similar than *both* candidate- and party-oriented campaigners; in 1984 the issue-oriented took honors in every domain other than domestic spending for having policy preferences *least* like those of the Democratic rank and file. Thus, the spending issue in 1984 provided the only instance in either year in which issue-oriented campaigning was associated with elite representation of mass policy sentiments.[2]

Although party and party faction may be the carriers of standing individual differences on matters of ideology and public policy preferences, delegates who wish to represent party interests in the proceedings of the nominating conventions or who are committed to doing party work more generally in campaigning are also delegates who are most representative of ordinary voters' issue positions and policy preferences. *Party indeed seems to provide a persistent linkage connecting the issue preferences of the partisan citizen to the policy commitments of the partisan elite.*

In electoral analyses, party is often played off against issue voting as a contrasting determinant of electoral decision-making. That may be appropriate, particularly where new policy alternatives disrupt established patterns of voting. However, it now seems quite evident that our understanding of the role of party in the process of presidential selection must lead to a generous recognition of the extent to which party binds leader to follower and structures the policy content of national political competition.

Party Organization

The role of party in linking mass aspirations to elite commitments has, as previously noted, many manifestations in the ongoing political process. One of these takes the familiar form of an organizational presence. The organizational manifestation of party is present in our study largely through one piece of information extracted from participating political activists: their assessments of the strength of the local party organization back home.

The referent for the appraisal differs in a number of ways from other assessments of party with which we are concerned but particularly in the specificity with which it suggests a linking mechanism connecting masses and elites. For instance, as noted earlier, without further probing it is impossible to know the precise referent for the elites' assertions of the strength of their party support. Individuals may have had in mind comparisons with any of a variety of norms in deciding "how strong" was their support for party, and the "party" that provided the focus for their campaign efforts may have been a local party, a state party, or some element of the national party. But such ambiguity does not pertain where "the party organization in your community" is concerned.

The geographic specificity of this query suggests another perspective on the measurement of mass-elite linkages, complementing the comparison of national means and the correlation of national distributions. The possibility of specific geographic linkage suggests the conceptual and analytic mode of representational analysis specified by the concept of "dyadic correlations."[3] Central to the concept is the simple fact that each delegate has some institutional links to one particular constituency and, therefore, to a specific subset of mass partisans. Given the institutional setting for the selection of delegates, each delegate is in fact a member of a state delegation that is uniquely linked to a state constituency.

The early representation studies in the mode of the original Miller-Stokes design took the congressional district (rather than the state) as the unit of analysis and analyzed the circumstances under which congressional candidates resembled or failed to resemble their district constituencies.[4] Both in Miller-Stokes and in the latest version of that design, the Converse-Pierce analysis of representation in the French assembly,[5] the fundamental concern was with the conditions that linked candidates to their own constituencies. The basic analytic objective in both studies was to discover conditions under which covariation in elite and mass attitudes was enhanced or inhibited. The analytic technique was the computation of a correlation based on the dyadic links between constituency and candidate.

In the literature on representation, the problem of measuring mass-elite linkages has been examined with some care, and a number of alternatives have been proposed. At one time or another, as in the present work, the analysis of representational linkage has rested on analytic groups consisting of national populations of political elites and national populations of rank-and-file partisans, treated in the manner introduced in Chapter 2. The summary of their positions as reflected by aggregate means is in common usage. Following the discussion provided by Robert Weissberg,[6] the comparisons of mass and elite have also been explored through the correlational measure of "collective representation" we have used here and that was also used in *Parties in Transition.*

The leading methodological critique of approaches using correlations based on dyadic comparisons of mass-elite linkages was provided by Christopher Achen.[7] His analysis was motivated by skepticism concerning the interpretation of the correlations used by Miller and Stokes in the early 1960s. Rejecting the use of such correlations because of fundamental flaws inherent in their interpretation, Achen suggested at least two alternative measures—which nevertheless took advantage of the information that could be obtained by pairing particular elite actors with specific subsets of rank-and-file constituents. In the present study we took advantage of some of Achen's suggestions. We treated the state as a basic unit of analysis, and we inquired into the match between state "delegations" of elite activists and state "constituencies" of rank-and-file partisans. The interpretable results of this analysis, however, rest on comparisons of state means and mean differences of mass and elite means, not on dyadic correlations.

In many respects, and quite apart from our present interest in local party organizations, it seems intuitively plausible to use the state as a basic part of our measurement procedure in exploring our version of mass-elite linkages. Although it is clearly true that some aspects of presidential politics are thoroughly nationalized, given that the candidacies involved are national, it is also true that the presidential selection process is constrained by our federal system of politics. Whether delegates to nominating conventions are elected in a primary or selected in a caucus or convention, they become part of a state delegation. And those who are the direct participants in this selection are at least nominally limited to choosing fellow residents of a given state.

Quite apart from the state of residence of the delegates, there remains a real sense in which the existence of the electoral college defines fifty separate state elections as the sites for the ultimate choice between party nominees for the presidency. Between the springtime selection of delegates and the fall election of a president, much of the campaign activity centers on individual state constituencies. It is clear that election strategies, from the selection of delegates on, are shaped in some substantial part to fit what are thought to be state-based differences among voters.

As Converse and Pierce recognized, there is much merit in the suggestions made by Achen—particularly when interstate, compared with intrastate, variance is limited. As a consequence, our analytic procedure was to pursue simultaneously four modes of assessing the match or congruence between mass and elite attitudes. As is already evident, (1) some of our comparisons are comparisons of national means derived from aggregating individual level data. The means we have reported so far have been for groups of individuals, where the mean is a group mean estimated by taking into account each individual contributing to the distribution of scores within the group. In similar fashion (2) the correlations we have used to assess similarity and dissimilarity have been derived by correlating individual data specifying status differences (such as elite versus mass) with individual attitudinal differences on each of our six measures. Just as the magnitude of group differences is reflected in the difference of their means, so the magnitude of the same differences is reflected in the extent to which the distributions of attitudes are correlates of the status differences, large correlations having the same meaning as large differences of means.

With the state as a subunit of aggregation for individual

data, (3) we also computed state-by-state means for each analytic subset of elites and have examined the differences, state
by state, between those means and the means derived for the
aggregates of Democratic and Republican partisans in each
state. In our exploratory analyses we have compared mean
differences of the state level elite means and mass means.
Finally, (4) we have also correlated the state means for subsets
of elites with the state means for partisan populations within
each state. This has meant a dyadic correlation of state elite
means with state mass means: in 1984, with thirty states, the
correlation matrix for dyadic comparisons had thirty entries
(properly weighted by sample size).

We have then compared all four indications of mass elite
similarities and differences. Three of the measures have proved
to be remarkably comparable across all of our analyses. The
"collective correlations" between pairs of national groups of
individuals and their attitudes, the comparison of national
group means, and the comparison of mean differences of state-
level differences in mass and elite means consistently lend
themselves to very similar interpretations. The fourth measure,
however, the dyadic correlation of the state-level means of
elites linked to the mean attitudes of state rank-and-file populations, have often revealed the lack of interpretability suggested by Achen.

In some analyses, all four measures of group similarities
and differences led to the same interpretation and the same
conclusions; in others, the consistency was limited to three
measures and did not include the dyadic correlation. Exploratory analyses have suggested that these were more often
than not instances in which the ratio of interstate variance to
intrastate variance was very low (eta's of less than .20),
suggesting instability in the estimates of state differences, particularly where the estimates were for populations of mass
partisans. Throughout the remainder of this book, our conclusions are based on the consistency with which group means
derived from individual data, group differences assessed by
correlating individual level data, and state-based means and

mean differences based on state-by-state comparisons of elites and masses lead to uniform interpretation. We have not attempted to reconcile these with dyadic correlations, and I will not report the numerous instances in which dyadic correlations appear to add further confirmation to the interpretation suggested by the other three measures. (Because this methodological decision was important to a number of our interpretations of data, the basic information about the ratio of interstate to intrastate variance is presented in Appendix A.)

In contrast to the sharp and rather uniform differences that we have seen associated with being a strong party supporter—emphasizing party in one's campaign efforts or representing party interests in convention—the perceived strength of party organization back home apparently makes only a modest contribution to mass-elite differences in either party. This well may be the case because in eliciting information about the party organization, our inquiry centered on the question of *local* party organizations. With the benefit of hindsight we would now presume that state organizations would better fit the institutional link between state-selected activists and bodies of state-defined party supporters. In any event, the available evidence does not suggest a significant role for local party organizations in linking elite opinion to mass opinion.

Among Democrats, comparisons of state means do suggest that strong local organizations link leaders and followers. We say "suggest" because the analytic differences are small, as are the differences in national aggregate means, which only suggest a tendency for elites coming from strong organizational settings to be more moderate and therefore more like the national Democratic rank and file. The correlational measures of elite-mass similarities are comparably ambiguous; only on the question of liberal/conservative identifications and on the indicator provided by attitudes toward spending for domestic programs do delegates associated with strong local party organizations clearly look more like the national Democratic constituency.

Among Republicans the picture is even less clear. Where

there are no instances of "contradictory" evidence among
Democrats, exactly nine of the eighteen tests (twelve comparisons of means and six of correlations) among Republicans
suggest that strong party organizations are dysfunctional for
the representation of mass partisan preferences. Given the national context described in Chapter 3, in which it seems that
those in control of the Republican party may have become
estranged from their rank-and-file supporters, it is tempting to
conclude that local Republican organizations as well as the
national Republican leadership have let ideological enthusi-
asms carry them afield from their base of electoral support.
Our data suggest that compared with the situation obtaining
for the Democratic party, this may be so—but the fragile nature
of our evidence and the absence of corroborating data foreclose
any firm conclusion. Local Democratic organizations may facilitate mass-elite linkages in some domains but not in others,
and local Republican organizations may inhibit as often as they
facilitate, but our evidence is limited on both counts.

Electoral Competition

If the representation of party electoral competition interests
in nominating conventions is an analogue to the representation
of party in government, and if party as organization is reflected
in the delegates' report on the strength of their local party
organizations, then party in the electorate may well be represented by the relative partisan competitiveness in electoral
strength. "Party in the electorate" usually refers to the incidence or the salience of partisan loyalties as determinants of
mass electoral behavior, but our interest was in one of the
consequences or derivations of the incidence of partisanship
of the voters. To the extent that the partisanship of voters
determines the long-term or standing division of the partisan
vote, it sets the context for all political competition, intraparty
as well as interparty.

Table 24. Elite Perceptions of Partisan Balance in Local Politics,
1984

Perception	Democrats	Republicans
Republicans dominant	33%	56%
Balanced competition	11	11
Democrats dominant	56	33
	100%	100%
Number of cases	920	839

Data not collected in 1980.

In order to examine the relative dominance of the party of
the elites in local partisan competition, in 1984 (only) we asked
each delegate to describe the competitive balance in his or her
local party politics. Democrats and Republicans gave remarkably similar descriptions, as depicted in Table 24. Identical
proportions of slightly more than half the activists in each party
reported that they came from areas in which their own party
was dominant; an even third in both parties reported that they
came from areas in which their party was in the minority and
the other party dominant; and almost precisely one in nine in
each party reported coming from an evenly balanced, competitive locale. Given these three alternatives defining the status
of each delegate's party, it is possible to define differences in
partisan context within which to examine similarities between
elites and masses.

One can look for two complementary but different sets of
results. First, a basic tenet of Democratic theory holds that
electoral competition should enhance the representativeness of
elected officials. Of course, other outcomes are possible. As
an example, one of the early investigations using the Miller-
Stokes paradigm for the study of representation in Congress
led to the conclusion that officials representing constituencies
in which their party was clearly dominant tended to resemble
their constituents precisely because, by virtue of their domi-

Table 25. Perceived Local Partisan Balance and Mass-Elite Similarities, 1984

Perception	Liberal Conservative		Social Issues		Foreign Policy		Domestic Spending		New Politics		Traditional Groups	
	Dem.	Rep.	Dem.	Rep.	Dem.	Rep.	Dem.	Rep.	Dem.	Rep.	Dem.	Rep.
Republicans dominant	+.33	−.29	+.53	−.16	+.41	−.19	−.15	−.57	+.18	−.33	+.37	−.56
Competitive party strength	+.20	−.15	+.40	−.03	+.28	−.08	−.08	−.39	+.12	−.20	+.26	−.34
Democrats dominant	+.32	−.26	+.47	−.15	+.41	−.18	−.10	−.51	+.16	−.27	+.35	−.51
Dominant vs. competitive	+12	+14	+07	+13	+13	+11	+2	+18	+4	+13	+9	+22
Minority vs. dominant	+1	−3	+6	−1	0	−1	+5	−6	+2	−6	+2	−5

Signs in the upper portion of the table indicate that elites are more or less conservative than are masses. In the second row from the bottom, the plus (+) signs indicate that elites from competitive areas are *more similar* to their party's mass supporters than are elites from areas in which their party is dominant. In the bottom row, the plus (+) signs indicate that elites from areas in which their party is dominant are *more similar* to their party's mass supporters than are elites from areas in which the opposition is dominant.

nance, the constituents made up very homogeneous constituencies that were easily represented by fellow partisans.[8]

In the present analysis we were not necessarily looking at elected officials, and our measures of interparty balance certainly had little to do directly with the *intra*party competition that produced the selection of our elites. Nevertheless, it is of more than passing interest that the evidence in Table 25 is unmistakable—and particularly on the Republican side—that activists from areas in which the parties are evenly balanced were much more like their fellow partisans in the mass electorate than were delegates elected from areas in which their own party is clearly dominant.

It is not altogether clear why this should be so. In a rough sense the evidence is consistent with the notion that competition encourages responsiveness to constituent demands and thereby enacts the Downsian law forcing political leaders to centrist positions more likely to command broad support. However, it is not completely obvious why Republican leaders from areas in which their rank-and-file supporters were dominant should resemble the national population of rank-and-file Republicans *less* than did Republican leaders from competitive areas. And yet with regard to all three measures employing both means and correlations, the generalization held across all six substantive domains. It is as though a developed sensitivity to rank-and-file demands, regardless of party, evokes more attention to fellow partisans as well as to the opposition. The uniformity of the findings may anticipate our next thesis and suggest that the absence of competition breeds irresponsibility—or occasions freedom of conscience—whether in the complacent majority or the hopeless minority.

The second set of comparisons explored this possibility by testing to see whether leaders selected in areas of their own party's greatest weakness were less constrained to follow their own party lines and were therefore less like their own rank and file than leaders selected where their party dominated the electoral scene. The evidence was different for the two parties.

With one exception, again in the domain of domestic spending, Democratic leaders from Republican-dominated locales exhibited means that were slightly *more liberal*—not more conservative—than those of other Democrats, and Table 25 shows that mass-elite dissimilarities among Democrats were also slightly greater in Republican areas on five of the six measures. In contrary fashion, however, there was a tendency for Republicans elected from Democratic districts *also* to be more liberal—not more conservative—than Republicans from areas in which their own party dominated (still excepting the issue of domestic spending).

Although we have no additional evidence on the point, these data are consistent with the thesis that Democratic party leaders in enemy territory *react* to the policies of the opposition and become somewhat more extreme advocates of their own party positions when their opposition dominates the electoral scene. It seems also to be true that Republicans from the most competitive areas, where they are most like the Republican rank and file, are marginally less extreme in their ideological position and score somewhat less strongly conservative than do their counterparts from Republican-dominated areas. Another difference between parties appears, however, because this theme of competition-induced *moderation* underlying the greater congruence did not hold for Democrats. On the Democratic side, leaders from competitive areas tended to be, if anything, a bit more liberal (more extreme) than Democrats from strongly Democratic locales. This leaves the possibility that the pronounced impact of competition on the accentuation of mass-elite similarities has more to do with a dominant culture of political responsiveness and motivation stemming from interparty electoral competition than it does with the direct mechanisms involved in delegate selection.

Party, then, is not the enemy of ideology in mass electorates; it is the principal carrier and organizer of mass issue preferences and helps provide a structure for national politics that articulates and integrates the issue concerns of leaders and followers. In its various circumstances and differing guises, it facilitates the matching of elite policy preferences with mass support for similar preferences. Sentiments prompted by personal feelings of party loyalty among elites may not bind them to their supporting masses, but elites who take their cues from party, whether in convention or in campaign, do exhibit greater than average rapport with the issue preferences of rank-and-file fellow partisans. The natural processes of ongoing presidential politics in both 1980 and 1984 sustained the primacy of party and its place in linking mass and elite policy preference.

5

Linkage Mechanisms: Ideological Factions and Issue Representation

Setting the discussion of the role of party in linking mass and elite policy preferences prior to a discussion of the consequences of elite representation of policy commitments provides another bit of irony from the analysis. We began our inquiry in 1972 wanting to learn more about what resulted from the various recent reforms of the presidential selection process. As our work evolved, we found evidence that reform priorities pertaining to the importance of questions of public policy produced only a temporary reduction of the central importance of party in Democratic presidential politics. This was part of a larger conclusion that time-honored competition for political power provides a marvelous countervailing force to efforts to reform and redirect the institutions involved in presidential selection.

In the previous chapter, we reviewed evidence indicating that the resurgence of devotion to party within the presidential elite is unmistakably relevant to the active promotion of mass policy preferences. Now, the discussion comes full circle to examine evidence produced by the basic dilemma facing political activists who are motivated by a commitment to promote policies and issue positions.

Issue Representation

At least in the mid 1980s, those most concerned with presenting or representing positions on matters of public policy were those most out of step with the issue sentiments of the partisan rank and file. This was particularly true, as one might expect, regarding the newest issues from domains in which leaders must almost by definition differ from a lagging, slow-to-respond constituency. It was also true, however, of more enduring, long-standing themes.

Our analysis began with two familiar arenas of political action, the nominating convention and the campaign. In the last chapter we commented at length on the correlates of sponsorship and representational forces in the nominating convention. Although our major concern was with party, we noted the repeated pattern in which issues were relegated to a minor place by most elite activists, particularly in the Republican party. It is true that early in the selection process, according to our reconstructions, delegates reporting sponsorship and assistance as they sought to become delegates considered special interests and issue groups virtually as prominent as the presidential candidates. This was not true for Republicans in 1980, when the contest for the nomination produced much more convention activity by the candidates, overshadowing the intervention of interest groups in the delegate selection process. In both the 1980 and 1984 conventions, subsequent delegate efforts to represent both party and candidates in convention decisions decisively outpaced their representation of issue groups. Although special-interest groups were second only to party in shaping the selection of delegates, in both years they fell behind in the incidence of influence as convention decision-making followed delegate selection. And in both years, delegates' comparative assessments of the general importance of pursuing party- or issue-oriented goals in the convention proceedings gave an unmistakable priority to party concerns or the preferences of the voters they represented.

The handful of Democrats at the 1984 convention who did represent the causes associated with such new social issues such as abortion, homosexuality, and affirmative action were not unique in reflecting a substantial lack of rapport with the policy preferences of rank-and-file Democrats. As noted in the discussion of Table 21 in the preceding chapter, in both 1980 and 1984 their peers who were representing candidate interests at the convention exhibited even greater dissimilarity with the issue preferences of the national population of Democrats. Nevertheless, Democrats who represented the new social issues were, in both years, quite remarkably more liberal than their colleagues in convention (to say nothing of the Democratic rank and file) and on all six indicators of ideology and policy preferences.

Democrats representing more traditional issues—including those pertaining to labor, agriculture, and education—were predictably more moderate in their issue preferences, but they provided only a modest improvement over the social-issue advocates when it came to matching partisan sentiments in the mass electorate. Although they were more like the masses than were the candidates' advocates, the data in Table 21 indicate that they did not match those representing the voters or party interests on any of our eleven indicators in 1980 and 1984—save one.

Although virtually all the Democratic elite matched rank-and-file sentiments concerning governmental spending for domestic programs in 1984, delegates concerned with representing issues—whether new social issues or traditional social welfare policies—were, by a good margin, most similar to national Democratic rank-and-file sentiments on the spending theme; they outdid all other categories of Democratic delegates on all three of our methods of measuring similarity on the question of domestic spending. Since the six-item measure of attitudes toward spending was the only measure in either year (1980 or 1984) on which the mass base of a party's support took a more extreme position than did the party elite, it is perhaps not surprising that the views of the ultraliberal delegates who were promoting issue causes turned out to be more similar to mass sentiments on this issue than were those of their colleagues.

In view of the prominence accorded the New Right in Republican politics, it is important to note that neither in 1980 nor in 1984 did more than a scattering of Republican delegates in our study report that their own quest for selection as delegates, or their subsequent efforts at representation in convention, involved the new social issues or the groups promoting a position (presumably conservative) on such issues. Indeed, there are not enough Republican representatives of social-issue groups in our study to permit even the most rudimentary analysis. This accords with evidence indicating that despite the 1972-80 transformation of the Republican elite into a very homogeneous ideological group, there seemed not to have been a commensurate increase in their campaign emphasis on the questions of public policy that united them in their support of Reagan.[1]

Republican representation of traditional special interests also lagged behind that of the Democrats, but there were enough persons in our study to permit some interesting generalizations about them in both 1980 and 1984. In 1980 the Republicans provided a sharp contrast to their Democratic counterparts, as can be observed in Table 21 (Chapter 4). Republicans representing traditional interest groups in the 1980 convention were somewhat more conservative than the party norm; nevertheless, the correlational estimates of their match with rank-and-file Republican attitudes in our five policy domains showed their preferences to be more generally similar to mass preferences than was true for Republicans representing either party or candidate. With some exceptions, the same conclusion was supported by evidence drawn from state-by-state comparisons of mass and elite differences. These pieces of evidence are at least consonant with the conclusion of electoral research that Reagan's election in 1980 was partially a consequence of national preferences for his (and the Republican party's) emphasis on more conservative national governmental policies.[2]

Four years later, circumstances had changed. Relative to the norms set by other Republican delegates, special-interest representatives in 1984 were much more conservative than the rest of their colleagues. Only on the question of spending for domestic programs were their attitudes visibly more moderate than those of the other Republican delegates. Thus, by 1984, issue-oriented Republicans found themselves in much the same situation as issue-oriented Democrats. Although their convention behaviors were guided, at least in part, by their commitment to represent organization points of view on questions relevant to public policy, their own issue preferences, among those we tapped for measurement, were not closely attuned to those of others in the party, and they were quite out of line with mass preferences. Only delegates preoccupied with representing their chosen candidates were like them in reflecting, or representing, mass opinions.

Proceeding chronologically from delegate selection to convention proceedings and on to the campaign, we again encountered the limited incidence of Republican concern with issues. In both 1980 and 1984 only one in twenty of the Republican elite reported that they participated in a presidential campaign "to work for an issue," as opposed to doing party work or being committed to a candidate. Therefore, in neither year is our base for analysis of Republicans very solid. It is, nevertheless, of interest at the most general level because it provides further support for some earlier conclusions.

In 1980, it seems that Republican activists who campaigned on behalf of issues consistently held issue preferences more like those of the Republican rank and file than was true either for party workers or for candidate supporters. In contrast to their peers who represented issue groups in convention, the issue campaigners apparently achieved their rapport with the Republican masses at least in part because they were visibly more moderate in their policy preferences. In all five domains they were less conservative than either the party people or the candidate people. Four years later, relative moderation had been replaced by absolute extremism, and while rapport with the rank and file did not dwindle into complete estrangement, those working for issues had lost their claim to being the most representative of the campaigners.

Among Democrats the record was clear and unchanging. Those campaigning on behalf of issues in 1980 were radically more liberal in each of the five domains. Overall, as a consequence (see Table 23, Chapter 4), they were least representative of mass Democratic sentiment. The campaign of 1984 produced a reprise except, once again, for the broad issue of preferred level for public expenditure: there was an extraordinarily close match between issue campaigners and the national Democratic rank and file in attitudes toward spending. This was the only break in an otherwise uniform set of results illustrating the gap between the issue preferences of the issue-oriented Democratic elite and those of their partisan support groups in the electorate.

The evidence for both parties in both years suggests an important challenge to would-be leaders in the fact that party regulars, against whom the issue-oriented reformers rebelled, consistently provided the stronger links between masses and elites, the greater incidence of representation of mass policy preferences. Meanwhile, ideological rebels—such as those who sought reform in the Democratic party, the better to represent "broad-based grassroots opinion"—may themselves be substantially out of line as representatives of mass opinion. Of course, the sins of those in the vanguard making new social policy should not be visited on their predecessors of earlier decades. Those who seek change in the name of the public's interest hope to lead opinion, and we should not expect to find them mirroring mass opinions about policies they are trying to change. The evidence reviewed so far certainly illustrates that representing public opinion involves a different relationship to that opinion than is involved in changing it.

This is not to say that the passive mirroring of public opinion
was characteristic of the political elites under investigation
here. Leaving the particulars of the elections of 1980 and 1984
and returning to the broader theme of inter- and intraparty
differences that introduced the discussion in the first chapter,
one immediately finds reflections of the dynamic nature of
contemporary party competition, with clear implications that
large changes are underway in the structuring of policy preferences.

Ideological Factions

Historically, both parties have contained recognized ideological factions that have persistently defined internal struggles
for the power associated with party leadership. At a later point
we will explore some of the correlates associated with the wings
of each party defined by the party leadership of the past four
decades. First, however, we need to examine intraparty differences defined by the contemporary self-identification of elites
as liberals, centrists, and conservatives. The foregoing chapters
have used the basic information on ideological identification
as a "dependent variable," a criterion variable for assessing
mass-elite similarities. Adding to the self-description, however—amending the base measure by incorporating elite perceptions of the ideological locations of other elite members of
the party—creates a new measure of intraparty elite differences.

In general, we define each party's left wing as made up
of self-designated *liberals* who (on a 7-point scale from liberal
to conservative) placed themselves at positions 1 or 2 *or* chose
a qualified liberal position, 3, but then located "the other delegates at the convention" at 5, 6, or 7 on the scale. *Centrists*
are 4s or 3s who put their fellow delegates at 1, 2, or 4, or 5s
who assigned their peers to 6, 7, or 4. The right wing is the
mirror image of the left. Only minor fragments of the left or

Table 26. Ideological Factions among Elites, 1984

Faction	Democrat	Republican
Left	41%	4%
Center	51	48
Right	8	48
	100%	100%
Number of cases	991	834

See Appendix C for an operational definition of the factions.

the right were 3s or 5s; these we called moderates unless they located their fellow partisans on the other side of the scale's midpoint.

With this emendation, the resulting ideological distributions within the parties remain remarkably dissimilar and belie the oft-repeated image of the American parties as "umbrella" parties. It is true that the distributions overlap, particularly in the middle categories of self-labeling. However, even at this first level of measurement (see Table 26) the different orientations of the parties are reflected in the fact that a full 40 percent of the Democrats but only 4 percent of the Republicans were self-described liberals, while only 8 percent of the Democrats shared the conservative label with almost 50 percent of the Republicans (roughly 50 percent in each party were self-designated centrists).

A more meaningful assessment of party differences is provided by summaries of the issue positions associated with this apparently overlapping use of ideological labels. Table 27 illustrates the general configuration to be found in the five issue domains covered by the 1984 study. Centrist Republicans are much more conservative on social issues than are centrist Democrats; they are in fact more conservative in their attitudes than are Democrats who call themselves conservative. Republican liberals, in turn, are scarcely distinguishable from Democratic centrists, and the other party groups—Democratic

Table 27. Policy Preferences of Ideological Factions among Elites, 1984

Ideological Faction	Social Issues		Foreign Policy		Domestic Spending		New Politics		Traditional Groups	
	Dem.	Rep.	Dem.	Rep.	Dem.	Rep.	Dem.	Rep.	Dem.	Rep.
Left	16*	29	6	27	23	42	29	41	11	57
Center	32	63	19	58	31	52	44	61	25	85
Right	57	78	37	80	41	61	63	69	54	95

Entries are means for party factions; see Appendix B for index construction and scoring.

liberals and Republican conservatives—simply have no "other party" counterparts at all. This displacement in ideological positioning of party factions is repeated in elite assessments of New Politics groups, although the range of factional differences is truncated by the relatively moderate positions of both Democratic liberals and Republican conservatives. Where the measures of foreign policy and domestic spending are concerned, the interparty differences are considerably more dramatic: Republican liberals score well to the right of Democratic centrists; Republican moderates are much more conservative than Democratic conservatives; there is no Republican faction that even remotely matches the Democratic liberals; and Republican conservatives have a complete monopoly on right field. The most extreme differences are found in the assessments of traditional partisan groups: all three groups are properly ordered within each party, but liberal Republicans are actually a bit to the right of Democratic conservatives.

Given the predominantly centrist locations of both sets of mass partisan supporters, the patterns of mass-elite similarities and dissimilarities associated with the elite means displayed in Table 27 are roughly predictable. Accentuating the differences first described in Chapter 2, liberal Democrats and conservative Republicans exhibited the greatest lack of similarity with their rank-and-file party partisans. There are a number of variants on the theme, however, and enough additional regularities to prompt scrutiny of the results in all five issue domains. The data are displayed in Table 28. Intraparty comparisons show that among each party's elite groups, liberal Democrats and conservative Republicans were generally least representative of their parties' mass followers. The one exception again concerns domestic spending. It will be remembered that on this issue alone the Democratic masses were more liberal (more supportive of increased governmental spending) than were all Democratic activists. It now appears that party followers were much more liberal in their attitudes toward spending than were either centrists or conservatives among the Democratic dele-

Table 28. Mass Similarities with Elite Ideological Factions, 1984

Ideological Faction	Social Issues		Foreign Policy		Domestic Spending		New Politics		Traditional Groups	
	Dem.	Rep.	Dem.	Rep.	Dem.	Rep.	Dem.	Rep.	Dem.	Rep.
Left	.66	.29	.54	.21	.06	−.13	.38	.11	.59	.09
Center	.44	.04	.38	.01	−.20	−.48	.00	−.26	.31	−.48
Right	−.05	−.36	.03	−.40	−.32	−.64	−.26	−.47	−.25	−.67

Entries are correlations between scores of elite members of party factions and their national party mass; the larger the correlation, the greater the difference in scores. Negative entries indicate the elite faction is more conservative than the party mass; positive entries indicate the elite are more liberal.

gates. However, liberal activists were very much like rank-and-file Democrats (r = .06) and slightly more liberal.

As a consequence of this juxtaposition of views, domestic spending was the only domain in which conservative Democratic activists were less similar to the Democratic masses than were liberal activists. Although the mirror-image counterpart to that generalization is sometimes muted on the Republican side—perhaps by less-than-stable estimates from the very small set of left-wing Republicans—the reverse generalization also seems warranted. The views of the more liberal among the Republican elite were more representative of Republican rank-and-file sentiments than were the views of the dominant conservative Republican leaders. Therefore, the generalization that the prototypic factions in each party, liberal Democrats and conservative Republicans, are not only less representative of their parties' mass sentiments than are the centrists among the elite; they are less representative of mass preferences than are the minor fragments of leadership who form the ideological opposition within each party's elite.

Given the limited size of the ideological opposition in each party elite, it is perhaps more pertinent, and a sharper commentary, to note that in all five domains and in both parties the centrists provided more rapport with the party's rank and file than did those in the dominant ideological wing.

In the basic interparty comparison, it is difficult to judge where the bulk of evidence lies on the question of which party's leadership is more representative of party supporters' sentiments. On social issues and foreign policy, conservative Republican leaders are somewhat closer to their party's base than are liberal Democrats to the Democratic rank and file. On the same issues the very numerous centrists in both parties provide a decisive edge for Republican elite leadership. The situation is almost perfectly reversed for the other three policy domains; Democratic liberals and centrists do better than Republicans, sometimes by small margins, in providing representation for the opinions of their respective party followers. A cautious if perhaps too cynical observer might conclude that the two parties share the honors of providing ideological leadership that does not match rank-and-file preferences. Given the ideological polarization, or displacement from mass sentiment of both parties, even self-defined centrists often reveal only limited rapport with the masses. Ironically, the clear political losers within each party elite provide the clearest representation for the preferences of party followers.

6

Linkage Mechanisms: Political Leadership

If the political parties may be designated as the carriers of mass ideology, presidential candidates have long personified the policy preferences and ideological postures of the parties. Of course, the politics of the Reagan era can aptly be described in the impersonal terms of the ideological conflicts of liberals and conservatives or the contribution to the intellectual debates over basic social policies made by ex-liberals turned neo-conservative. Whatever the terms, there is little question that the quality of elite participation in presidential politics was fundamentally altered by the successful protests of the 1960s and 1970s. That turbulent period changed American domestic as well as foreign policy. It warmed the chill of McCarthyism and the Cold War, and it eventually spurred the response of the New Right to the successes if not excesses of the aroused left. The ideological dormancy of the Eisenhower years, in which intellectuals debated "the end of ideology," was succeeded by the sometimes strident articulation and confrontation of arguments over new policies, over social issues in particular.[1]

The debates of the 1980s were not particularly abstract in their origins. Gender and racial equality were sought in very concrete terms. Religious concerns were made manifest in very specific discussions of public policy concerning the basic institutions of the family, the church, and the schools. Beyond a near panic over the control of drugs, an increasingly sensitized population wrestled with the capacity of medical intervention to terminate and to prolong life.

Candidates for political leadership have inevitably been associated with the issues of the day: a woman candidate for vice-president, and a black candidate for president; a George McGovern championing the dispossessed and powerless; a Ronald Reagan carrying the challenging banner of the New Right; a benign Dwight Eisenhower reluctantly dealing with racial conflict and voluntarily expressing concern over the rise of a military-industrial complex shaping American national policy; a Lyndon Johnson bullying the nation to accept his vision of the Great Society.

Associations like these have made more public the fact that politics is always highly personal, a contest of individuals seeking and wielding power. Such contests are, indeed, much of the substance of political history, even without a continuing sense of impending crises. In the design of the 1984 study we attempted to capture some portion of the recent history of national party leadership by asking our elite activists to assess a series of partisan leaders, all candidates for or holders of national offices. We included all presidential candidates from both parties since 1952; we added Democrats Geraldine Ferraro, John Glenn, Gary Hart, Jesse Jackson, and Ted Kennedy, and Republicans George Bush, Robert Dole, and Jack Kemp to represent figures of current interest. We did not attempt to collect the detailed information that would have been necessary to reconstruct particular patterns of candidate preference. Instead, we simply sought measures of current affect—of the like or dislike for each leadership figure. The analysis of mass-elite linkages reported here is based on one of the discernible patterns of responses from our delegates.

Leadership Patterns

Within each partisan delegate group, Democrat or Republican, we examined the interrelationships of attitudes toward the relevant set of partisan leaders. In each party there were two dominant clusters of evaluations, and among the Democratic elite two additional patterns appeared. First of all, among the Democrats our analysis indicated two sets of four candidates who were evaluated similarly by our delegates and who thereby define the party's two dominant leadership wings. One set consisted of Jimmy Carter, Hubert Humphrey, Lyndon Johnson, and Walter Mondale; the other included Ferraro, Jackson, Kennedy, and McGovern. Interestingly, both Adlai Stevenson and John Kennedy were moderately associated with *both groups* but clearly did not belong with either, were not joined together by shared assessments, and were not treated separately in the analysis. However, another pair consisting of Glenn and Hart *were* joined together in a third distinct pattern. Although evaluations of Hart showed a very mild negative relationship to those of Democratic centrists and an equally mild positive association with the Democratic left, while assessments of Glenn exhibited exactly the opposite pattern, these two losing candidates were linked together in our factor analysis as a pair not included in either of the dominant wings of the party.

With the two dominant wings identified, we then compared individual delegates' average scores for all candidates associated with each of the two wings. Delegates could be classified as being more favorable to one wing or the other, or about equally supportive of both. However, an inspection of the distributions of assessments led us to create a fourth group of delegates consisting of all whose overall average appraisal of the left-wing leadership was, in absolute terms, negative: that is, a score of less than 50, where 50 indicates indifference and anything higher than 50 indicates some degree of positive regard. Hence, we have a left wing that preferred Ferraro, Jackson, Kennedy, and McGovern; a conservative wing that absolutely rejected the left wing; a centrist wing that preferred Carter, Humphrey, Johnson, and Mondale without rejecting the left wing; and a left-of-center wing that was equally favorable to both the left and the center.

Table 29. Democratic Ideological Factions and Leadership Wings,
1984

Faction	Left Wing	Left of Center	Centrist	Conservative
Liberal	73%	51%	30%	3%
Moderate	26	46	66	66
Conservative	1	3	4	26
	100%	100%	100%	100%
Number of cases	173	291	221	197
Relative size	20%	33%	25%	22%

The distribution of each of the four resulting groups of delegates on the measure of ideological factionalism (developed in the last chapter) is presented in Table 29, where it appears that our association of delegates with the leadership wings of the party has identified four quite different groups. In the left wing are those who not only preferred the leadership of the left but who, in three cases out of four, also saw themselves as liberals when asked to define their own ideological position. At the other extreme are conservative Democrats who both rejected the party's liberal leaders and constituted most (68 percent) of the party's self-proclaimed conservatives. In between are the left-of-center contingent—equally supportive of the left wing and the centrists—and the centrists themselves, most of whom (66 percent) located themselves at the center of the ideological spectrum.

The classification of Democratic elites in terms of their attitudes toward various wings of the party's national leadership is not simply different from the classification by ideological faction; it provides an added perspective from which to judge the party's ideological center of gravity. Until now the picture has been that of a Democratic party dominated by self-proclaimed liberals who have continued to move to the left even as the national presidential vote swings to the right. This characterization is substantially modified if we note the very bottom

Table 30. Republican Ideological Factions and Leadership Wings, 1984

Faction	Moderate	Centrist	Conservative
Moderate	8%	2%	1%
Center	71	42	22
Conservative	21	56	78
	100%	100%	100%
Number of cases	293	370	171
Relative size	35%	44%	21%

row in Table 29 and observe that the left wing of the Democratic party attracts no more than one in five of the party's presidential campaign elite; it is equaled in size if not outnumbered by self-proclaimed conservatives. The conservatives, in turn, are joined by another 25 percent in preferring something other than left-wing leadership. Although liberals outnumber conservatives, the left wing is not representative of the ideological balance within the party; the party is, in fact, dominated by moderates and centrists. None of this changes the earlier discussion of the continued move to the left; it does suggest a different dynamic to be worked out as leadership groups next contest for power.

Among Republican elites the configuration of leadership preferences is less complex (see Table 30). Republican delegates also identify with one of two leadership wings: a moderate wing includes Eisenhower, Gerald Ford, Bush, and Dole; a conservative wing joins Barry Goldwater, Richard Nixon, Reagan, and Kemp. This clustering of evaluations was intuitively predictable, but the results at the next stage, assigning delegates to one or the other wing, were somewhat surprising. Although almost half of the activist Republican delegates (44 percent) gave equally high marks to both leadership wings, the magnitude of the dominance of moderates (35 percent) over conservatives (21 percent) is quite out of line with our previous estimate of the relative numbers of ideological conservatives.

Table 31. Elite Policy Preference Scores for Leadership Wings, 1984

Candidate Preference	Liberal/ Conservative	Social Issues	Foreign Policy	Domestic Spending	New Politics	Traditional Groups
Democrats						
Left wing	19	19	4	24	30	15
Left of center	27	22	9	26	33	16
Centrist	34	30	16	28	40	18
Conservative	50	44	31	38	55	39
Republicans						
Moderate	63	60	56	52	59	83
Centrist	75	72	72	55	66	91
Conservative	83	81	80	63	69	93

Entries are mean scores for leadership wings; see Appendix B for index construction and scoring.

The easy characterization of the Republican party as dominated by a unified ideological right wing is thus sharply modified,
at least on the basis of the evaluations of party leaders who are
clearly aligned with either a centrist or conservative faction. The
moderate Eisenhower-Ford wing is almost twice the size of the
conservative Goldwater-Reagan wing, and it is as overwhelm-
ingly moderate or centrist (79 percent) as the supporters of the
right-wing leaders are ideologically conservative (78 percent).

Nevertheless, at first glance it seems that the differences in
the policy preferences and predispositions of delegates who have
been assigned to various leadership wings are very similar to the
differences among ideological factions observed in Chapter 5.
Given the implicit ideological differences of the two parties'
leadership wings, this is not surprising; indeed, it is reassuring
to have validation of the conventional conclusions about the ideological infrastructure of the intraparty contests for power.

Beyond this, however, differences between the juxtaposition
of ideological factions and among leadership wings provide important commentaries on the ideological structure of American
politics. In the first place, although the dominant leadership
wings—left wing and centrist for the Democrats, moderates or
conservatives for the Republicans—are clearly differentiated by
the policy preferences of their elite activists, the differentiation
is an attenuated version of the differentiation specified by the
ideological factions. Even if the conservative Democratic wing
is thought to anchor the non-left leadership ranks of the Democratic Party, the intraparty differences between them and the
Democratic left wing, as displayed in Table 31 (an average of
24 points on the six measures), are less than those between the
liberal and conservative factions in Table 27 (averaging 33 points
on the same measures). The contrast among Republican elites is
even greater. Across the six measures of policy preference, the
moderates' average scores are 40 points more liberal than those
of the conservative faction; the contrasting leadership wings differ
by an average of only 16 points.

With legitimacy as party elites deriving from loyalty to leaders

Table 32. Mass Linkage with Leadership Wings, 1984

	Democrat				Republican		
	Left Wing	Left of Center	Centrist	Conservative	Moderate	Centrist	Conservative
Ideology	.48	.42	.26	−.08	−.05	−.34	−.41
Social issues	.57	.57	.42	.18	.11	−.21	−.33
Foreign policy	.46	.48	.34	.12	.02	−.26	−.32
Domestic spending	.03	−.03	−.11	−.35	−.47	−.55	−.62
New politics	.30	.27	.10	−.25	−.19	−.40	−.38
Traditional groups	.43	.46	.41	−.05	−.39	−.59	−.53

Entries are correlations between scores of elite members of leadership wings and their national party mass; the larger the correlation, the greater the difference in scores. Negative entries indicate the elite wing is more conservative than the party mass; positive entries indicate the elite are more liberal.

rather than commitment to ideas, and with leaders being chosen to contest in a Downsian context for national favor, the differences between leadership wings are constrained more than is true where ideology structures the coalitions. The average difference of 16 points separating the moderate wing from the conservative wing of the Republican party, and only 9 points separating Democratic centrists from the Democratic left wing, underscore the earlier comments about the relative homogeneity of each party's elite in 1984.

As a complement to these intraparty differences, the same data document the extent to which party leadership channels intra-elite differences of ideological outlook into interparty differences. Where Table 27 presented evidence of some overlap between the two parties—often with liberal Republican factions roughly matching the preferences of Democratic centrists, and Republican centrists looking like Democratic conservatives—there is absolutely no overlap where leadership wings are concerned. In each of the six domains of policy preference assessed in Table 31, the most liberal leadership wing of the Republican elite is more conservative than the most conservative Democratic wing. With the correlations between faction and wing considerably less than perfect in either party, it seems that both ideological commitment and loyalty to party leadership influence the predisposition and preferences of the elite activists. And the complementarity of their association with policy preferences is reflected in their combined contribution to party differentiation.

It also contributes to mass-elite linkages. The data describing mass-elite similarities for the various leadership wings of each party are presented in Table 32. The table is arranged differently from others in order to make two points more evident. For all practical purposes there are two distinct patterns, prototypically displayed in the top row, from left to right. The first, evident for all preference measures except that pertaining to domestic spending, emphasizes the greater similarity of elite-to-party mass preferences in the center of the array (the lower correlations between group and preference differences) and the evidence of maximum dissimilarities at the two extremes.

The second point concerns the directional differences associated with the comparison of leadership wings and party masses. The largest positive correlations at the left of the table signify the extent to which the elite group is more liberal than its party's mass base; the point at which (moving from left to right) one encounters a negative correlation is the point at which the elite group is more conservative than its mass base. It is rare for the most liberal wing of the Republican party to be as liberal as the Republican electoral base; it is equally rare for conservative Democrats to match the liberal center of gravity of the Democratic rank and file. But both exceptions occur in the important domains of social issues and foreign policy.

Beyond these indications of regularity in the structure of elite, candidate-oriented differences, Table 32 also offers a somewhat different perspective on the representativeness within each party of the dominant wing. There is no major modification of the previous description on the Republican side, although the contrast between moderates and conservatives is rather dramatically represented. Not only are the moderate wing-Republican mass linkages much, much closer, but in only three of the six domains is the moderate elite notably more conservative than the mass.

On the Democratic side, however, one can recognize that the linkage between the dominant centrist Mondale wing and its mass base compares more than favorably with the dominant conservative-mass linkage on the Republican side. Only on the theme of contemporary social issues are the prime supporters of the Democratic nominee of 1984 less in tune with their party base than are the strongest supporters of President Reagan with the Republican base. At the same time, the Democratic conservative wing is clearly more representative of rank-and-file preferences than is Mondale's center wing on four of the six indicators, including social issues and foreign policy, where even the conservatives are more liberal than the Democratic mass.

Party Leadership in the 1980s

The accumulated importance of the contests over party leadership for the ideological structuring of presidential politics becomes apparent when one looks at the major presidential candidacies of the 1980s. The first chapters of this volume opened the discussion by highlighting contemporary intra- and interparty differences in mass-elite policy preferences. We described, if no more than in passing, the sharp conflicts over national policy that produced two decades of reform in the process of presidential selection and set the stage for the ideologically oriented elections of the 1970s and 1980s. When one examines the presidential candidacies of the period in greater detail, the context provided by the foregoing description and discussion of the issue preferences of activists associated with different wings of their respective parties gives a somewhat different cast to one's commentary on the contemporary scene. In essence, our conclusion is that even the highly ideological candidacies of the 1980s did not always plumb the depths of the divisions and schisms that permeate the contemporary party system. They may have contributed to the perpetuation of some interparty differences, and they may have accentuated some intraparty differences, but many of the comparisons between particular contemporary candidate support groups among our elite activists were pale reflections of differences in policy preferences and mass-elite linkages associated with the enduring ideological factions or time-honored leadership wings of the two parties. This was particularly true in 1984, albeit for somewhat different reasons in each party. In that year the intraparty divisions among Democrats were virtually unrelated to underlying ideological schisms, and among Republicans the Reagan incumbency obscured potential disagreements over similar matters of basic policy.

In 1980 the sharp intraparty differences among supporters of the leading contenders were clear reflections of traditional disagreements of long standing. Although the leading candidates, Carter and Reagan, won nomination quite handily, Ken-

Table 33. Issue Preferences of Candidate Support Groups, 1984

	Liberal/ Conservative	Social Issues	Foreign Policy	Domestic Spending	New Politics	Traditional Groups
Democrats 1980						
Carter	39	38	42		20	26
Kennedy	23	26	28		10	13
Democrats 1984						
Hart	30[1]	26	13	30	38	23
Jackson	28	34	15	20	35	24
Mondale	31	27	14	27	39	16
Republicans 1980						
Reagan	68	73	81		66	92
Other	55	52	64		35	80
Republicans 1984						
Reagan	74	71	71	57	66	91
Other	69	67	63	51	61	86

[1]Entries are mean scores for candidate support groups among the elites; see Appendix B for index construction and scoring.

nedy supporters disagreed as sharply with the pro-Carter activists as left-wing elites disagreed with centrist elites in our analysis of historical patterns; and Reagan supporters differed from the John Anderson-Howard Baker-George Bush activists by margins generally characteristic of enduring moderate-conservative disagreements. At the same time, because the Carter camp of 1980 was quite conservative as centrist Democrats go, and despite the right-wing fervor of many Reaganites, the Carter-Reagan differences were not more pronounced than the more general differences between Democratic centrists and Republican conservatives.

Four years later, as Table 33 reflects, Reagan's dominance had virtually eliminated the articulation of opposition within the Republican party. In the privacy provided by the act of filling out our questionnaire, a minority of Republican delegates chose another party leader rather than Reagan—but even so, their issue preferences were much more conservative versions of the moderate (Anderson-Baker-Bush) preferences in earlier years. The more general moderate-conservative differences that we earlier noted between historical leadership wings at an average of 16 points (on the 0-to-100 scale) had persisted in 1980 as an 18-point difference between the Reagan and the Anderson-Baker-Bush people; the same measure of differences in issue preferences dropped to the 5-point average in Table 33 for differences between those more and less supportive of Reagan in 1984.

The disappearance of policy disagreements among Democratic candidate support groups in 1984 was equally striking. Table 33 documents the virtual identity of the issue preferences of the supporters of Hart and Mondale, and it discloses a perhaps surprising lack of uniqueness in the policy preferences of Jackson supporters. The liberal qualities that placed Jackson in the left wing in the previous analysis are here apparent only on the theme of governmental spending for domestic programs. Elsewhere, the issue preferences of his supporters are distinctive only in the social issue domain, which includes busing as

Table 34. Mass Similarities with Elite Candidate Support Groups, 1984

Preferred Candidate	Liberal/ Conservative	Social Issues	Foreign Policy	Domestic Spending	New Politics	Traditional Groups
Democrat						
Hart	.35	.53	.42	−.17	.19	.31
Jackson	.23	.26	.23	.10	.14	.17
Mondale	.37	.51	.44	−.06	.18	.50
Republican						
Reagan	−.33	−.17	−.25	−.58	−.36	−.59
Other	−.18	−.05	−.10	−.46	−.23	−.47

Entries are correlations between scores of elite members of candidate support groups and their national party mass; the larger the correlation, the greater the difference in scores. Negative entries indicate the elite wing is more conservative than the party mass; positive entries indicate the elite are more liberal.

one of four specific components. Despite that inclusion, the elites supporting Jackson appear somewhat more *conservative* than the elite supporters of Hart and Mondale. This superficially perplexing finding may be more understandable when one remembers that Jackson is the Reverend Jesse Jackson with a visible part of his support coming from church- and family-oriented middle-class followers. Nevertheless, the Jackson elite appears less liberal than might have been expected.

The strong impression of intraparty homogeneity on policy preferences within both parties in 1984 is reinforced by mass-elite comparisons (see Table 34). There were, however, two notable exceptions of some possible political significance. First, among the Democrats, Jackson's supporters showed up quite consistently, and at times strikingly, as most like the national Democratic rank and file in issue preferences and policy predispositions. In particular, their relatively conservative posture on social issues was accompanied by a dramatic edge over other candidate support groups in their congruence with mass preferences in this domain. At the same time, their liberal stance on spending did not leave them disadvantaged in matching rank-and-file preferences so much as it produced the one situation in both parties in which an elite support group was more liberal—more in favor of increased governmental spending for domestic programs—than was the party rank and file. In the other four domains the clear evidence of rapport between Jackson's elite support group and the party's base of mass support suggests more potential political strength than his 1984 convention support might have indicated.

The Hart and Mondale support groups among the Democratic elite were as much like each other in relationship to the Democratic voters as they were like each other in their issue and policy preferences. One minor exception involves the Mondale supporters' closer match with rank-and-file partisans on the spending question—because of strong Mondale elite support for spending; a more significant exception is found in the substantial remove of Mondale supporters' preferences from popular attitudes toward traditional political groups. Some vestige of the 1984 campaign charge against Mondale— that he was involved with "special interests"—is visible here because the differences in mass and elite attitudes toward labor unions played a decided role in this disparity of mass-elite opinions.

The comparisons of mass-elite similarities among Republicans are notable largely in the extent to which the correlations accentuate evidence of the persistence of intraparty schisms. The measures of mass-elite similarities are, nevertheless, simply consonant with the differences in elite group means. Just as the differences in mean scores among elite candidate support groups were reduced from an average of 18 points in 1980 to 5 points in 1984, the difference in correlations measuring mass-elite dissimilarity dropped from an average of 26 in 1980 to 13 in 1984; the Reaganites did not greatly change their level of rapport with the Republican electorate at large, while the non-Reagan minority moved slightly away from the party's mass base.

Our reliance on data from 1984 to describe the diminution of intraparty disagreements in comparison with 1980 is doubly important precisely because the same 1984 data document the persistence of interparty difference and the potential for the articulation of factional disputes. Even though the data indicate that few Republican elite activists would admit to a preference for some party leader other than Reagan in 1984, and even though the data suggest that Hart and Mondale supporters of 1984, in particular, almost appeared to have agreed not to disagree, the ideological factionalism discussed in the previous chapter and the differentiation of historic leadership wings introduced in the first part of this chapter were both documented with the same data from the same election period. And we believe both general conclusions to be true: Any given election may produce candidates for party leadership whose presence gives the appearance of great party homogeneity; at the same time, basic differences in orientation, associated either with independent philosophic and ideological origins or with traditional and established lines of party leadership, will persist.

Given the stolid nature of public opinion and the multiplicity of causes of mass voting behavior, one can scarcely fault election campaign strategies that emphasize or deemphasize a candidate's policy preferences and, therefore, the distinctiveness of supporters' preferences. Or, with a different causal model in mind, one must anticipate candidates rising in popularity as different elite appraisals of the importance of ideological distinctiveness dominate the extended process of presidential selection. We have argued elsewhere that Carter's nomination followed the first of these strategies, resting on the mobilization of new elites with distinctly conservative preferences, and that Reagan's nomination followed the second model as he persuaded the core Republican elite of the acceptability as well as the desirability of his ideological preferences.[2] The lesson of 1984 is that the particulars of any given election may be epiphenomena where the basic ideological structure of the political system is concerned, but in the longer run it will still be political leaders, not party bureaucracies or political ideologies, that shape partisan ideologues and define the national policy agenda.

7

Linkage Mechanisms: Elite Orientations

Thus far in the discussion we have been restrained in our use of the language of political representation to describe the results of our study of mass-elite linkage—emphasizing instead the more strictly descriptive themes of similarities or dissimilarities between masses and elites. We have done so despite the fact that the nominating process is clearly a political institution designed to provide representation of a broad array of public interests in the process of presidential selection. We have been restrained because the selection of delegates is seldom made according to procedures and within structures normally associated with processes that are intended to create representation. Delegates, who become campaign activists, are seldom discussed in either the popular or the academic literature with regard to representational roles that go beyond representing support for particular candidacies. Perhaps because they are seen only as intermediaries in a process connecting the citizenry to the elected representatives of the polity, little is said about their role in representing concerns that are not directly identified with a specific candidate.

As Jeane Kirkpatrick points out in her insightful and immensely instructive discussion of delegates as representatives, even the efforts of the last two decades to reform the presidential selection process paid little attention to questions of representation beyond the obvious concerns with broadening participation to better "represent" various potential candidacies or selected demographic characteristics of the electorate.[1] Although broadening participation and involvement in the presidential selection process would seem filled with implications for the representational role of the nominating convention decision-makers, most discussion (other than Kirkpatrick's) has had a very narrow concern with demographic and procedural representativeness rather than substantive representation.[2] Thus the Democratic party commitment to increase access and broaden citizen participation in the process of presidential selection focused very heavily on making sure that blacks, women, and young people were present in "proper" proportions, and that occasions for delegate selection were sufficiently well publicized and so located as to permit all interested persons to attend and participate.

From all accounts, it seems thoroughly reasonable to conclude that the presumably higher goals being sought in broadening the base of participation, particularly in the Democratic party, were in fact promoted because they were identified with very specific candidacies. With the name of the game being the competition for nomination, the rules of the game were reshaped and reformed in the 1970s in order to alter the opportunities for the demonstration of support for one or another candidacy. Although much of the discussion of party reform is couched in noble terms of equity and justice and fairness, the acceptability of new rules—such as those establishing quotas for gender, race, and age, or establishing thresholds for minority representation—was directly linked to the consequences of advantaging or disadvantaging specific candidacies. For us, the point is less to argue whether the personal contest for political power should be so openly translated into new institutional forms than to note that so little of the discussion has been cast in terms of representation that is not intrinsically defined by the competition of candidacies or, traditionally, by the quest for power of individual party leaders.

Some Thoughts on Representation

The theoretical literature on representation in Democratic institutions is largely focused on the relationship between the rank-and-file citizenry and ultimate governmental decision-makers. When applied to congressmen, presidents, or even members of the judiciary, the very definition of representation embodies a rich array of considerations. However, when applied to the process of selecting those who will then select the decision-makers, rather than to the decisions themselves, it is less common for notions of representation to be used beyond treating with the political implications to be read into the results of the candidates' contests for power. Again, where the discussion does return to the mass base of politics, it is usually with a concern for ensuring that classes of individuals, such as union members or party leaders or the young, are somehow adequately represented (numerically) in the process of choosing among candidates.

The fact that nominating conventions do not themselves make final decisions about public policy should not limit discussion of the extent to which those who are nominated will represent one or another policy or value. But the fact that it is the presidential nominee who may make the ultimate decision has largely obscured serious consideration of the extent to which the nominators are themselves a link facilitating the transmission of values and policy preferences from the bottom to the top. Despite the absence of elaborated and well-articulated representational roles for delegates that go beyond submitting their candidate preferences to a decision-making arena, our studies have shown that there are systematic variations in the degree to which differing sets of delegates "represent," if only inadvertently, the attitudes, evaluations, and preferences of the mass electorate.

Kirkpatrick's discussion draws a distinction between representation as the end product of a process and representativeness as a matter of similarity, whether deliberately sought or not. Representativeness is assessed by comparing distributions of the relevant attributes exhibited by the elite and the mass. This is very much like the ideas of similarity and dissimilarity measured by our differences of means or our collective correlations. Although her discussion does not treat the questions explicitly, Kirkpatrick leaves the implication that the outcome of an effective representation process should be the creation of an elite that is representative of the mass. And though she does not actually specify, it sounds very much as though the process of creating representation must be a deliberate process "intended" to produce a match between the electorate's preferences or demands and the elites' preferences or decisions. Nothing is said about the possibility of processes that inadvertently, or as a by-product, enhance the "representativeness" of the elite. It is thus by implication a thesis that democratic representation is the intentional outcome of an institutionalized process.

The several ambiguities one encounters in trying to relate the status and function of delegates to the literature on representation can be traced to such theories of representation as that presented in Kirkpatrick's admirable summary of the concept:

In the democratic tradition the concept of representation is firmly associated by theory and practice with the doctrines of consent[3] and accountability and the institutions of popular elections and political parties. It is with that tradition that we are here concerned.[4] The basic tenets of the doctrine of democratic representation are:

First, that laws should be made not merely in the name of the community, but by persons selected in periodic, competitive elections by some large, specified portion of the adult members of the community (e.g., a majority or plurality) to represent them in a specified context (e.g., Congress, a state legislature) for the performance of some specified (and therefore limited) functions.

Second, that political representation requires the representation of the opinions of individual citizens.

Third, that the responsiveness of representatives to the will of citizens can be assured by frequent periodic elections which (a) limit the tenure of representatives and (b) hold them accountable to those who elected them or the quality of their representation.[5]

In primary elections, delegates may well obtain the limited consent of those who select them. Apart from primary elections, those who anoint the delegates may in turn rest their legitimacy on those who consented to *their* prior selection as party leaders, caucus organizers, and the like; nevertheless, the relevant consent at each level has to do primarily, if not solely, with support for a specific presidential candidate. The objective in broadening participation in delegate selection was to ensure that more people—more interests—could voice their consent (or denial) to the support of given candidacies. The literature, including Kirkpatrick's discussion, is silent on the precise question of whether those who consent to have a delegate represent their candidate preference have really consented to anything beyond that.

And if "consent" as a crucial element in theories of democratic representation is not articulated beyond the substantive realm of candidate support, "accountability" as a second crucial element has been similarly ignored in discussions of the nomination process concerned with representation. Accountability apparently exists largely in the implicit threat of future political sanctions to be levied on individuals by others—not necessarily those who selected the delegate as their representative in the first place. Nevertheless, it is clearly a topic of great concern to the rulemakers: witness the excitement generated by the Kennedy challenge to rule F(3)(C) in the Democratic convention of 1980. The rule had transformed any uncertainty about accountability by making committed delegates accountable to their preferred choices among the candidates; it authorized their chosen candidate to replace them should their agreement falter under the pressure of new circumstances. But this, again, is clearly accountability only to a candidate and to formal participation in the declaration of a candidate preference. The candidate preference of those who elect a delegate might change as winter passes into spring and the campaign suggests a new candidate better able to carry the flag for the issues that mobilized the delegate's support in the first place. But none of the contemporary discussions about presidential selection, and few of the rules governing the process, are shaped for delegates who would switch candidates in order to remain true to their ideological commitments or to their representation of those who selected them.[6]

To the extent that these observations are valid, it is difficult to describe and discuss convention delegates in the established and familiar terms of representation theory. And yet, if one is concerned to understand the processes that link the preferences of the governed to the choices of the governors, the role of the convention delegate as campaign activist is demonstrably relevant to the effective functioning of presidential selection as an institutionalized process of representation. It would seem that our normative theories of representation should be expanded to accommodate these, and perhaps other, demonstrations of the inadvertent consequences of political action.

There is a second way in which the orthodox treatments of representation, such as those of Kirkpatrick, seem constrained. Representativeness seems to have to do only with the attributes of the mass polity. Little consideration is given to the idea of representing interests other than those of individuals. Kirkpatrick does make reference to the extent to which current democratic theory emphasizes the individual as opposed to the organized social units that might be represented in corporatist theory, but she discusses the matter as though the two are incompatible or at least incongruent.[7]

It would seem reasonable to develop theories of democratic society that emphasize the different representational functions being performed in the name of quite different entities. These could involve the party to be represented in the interest of partisan success, or party to be represented in the interest of a party ideology based on process or structure rather than governmental policy. The representation of candidacies might focus on those personal qualities of integrity or competence or morality that need not be attributes of the party or of ideology so much as attributes of national leadership. It should also be possible to think of representing policy alternatives that are not necessarily embodied either in party platforms or in specific candidacies. In short, it would seem quite reasonable to develop a democratic theory of pluralistic society in which different actors and groups of actors perform different essential functions, all of which should be "represented" in the selection of political leadership. If there are such roles for parties or candidates or interest groups that are intended to serve societal purposes beyond the immediate interest of the individual voter, it could then follow that representation should involve a match with something other than rank-and-file partisan sentiments in questions of ideology or public policy.

In fact, in virtually all the empirical studies, representation is taken to mean only the match of elite policy sentiments with the issue sentiments of some aggregation of individual voters.[8] In this analysis we have made no attempt to assess the relative success or failure of those delegates who are attempting to represent some aspect of party *rather than* voters' issue preferences, or special-interest issue preferences rather than those of party or voter; our only criterion of representativeness involves the similarity or dissimilarities of elite sentiments and rank-and-file sentiments.

From this perspective, one must interpret our analysis of delegates' representational goals or their styles of convention decision-making as producing variations in the extent to which any attempt to represent party, candidate, issues, groups, or voters ends up being associated with different degrees of representativeness measured *only* in terms of representing voter preferences. This limited portrayal of representation ignores the goals that delegates may be seeking and assesses their success with the singular criterion of providing representativeness for citizens' policy preferences.

At the same time, side by side with institutions designed to promote the goals of party candidate or interest group there exist normative perspectives that take their institutional form from theories of representation that specify different preferences for the ideal relationship between representatives and the larger community.

Representative Roles

Both in 1980 and in 1984 we explored the possibility that delegates carried with them, as we presume most politicians do, a sense of whether it is more appropriate to act in accordance with the wishes of others or in response to one's own independent judgment. With a narrow focus on the nominating convention as the setting for decision-making—although not necessarily the setting for an independent decision as to the nomination—we asked delegates and former delegates about their approach to decision-making: "On a scale of 1 to 7, with '1' being vote the way I believe is right, regardless of what the people I represent believe, and '7' being vote the way those people would vote if they were here, regardless of what I believe, where would you place yourself in regard to your role as a delegate decision-maker?" The choice was thus between voting the way "I think" is right and voting the way "the people I represent" would vote.

Although perhaps a leading question, in presuming that every respondent had a referent in mind for "the people I represent," the query's scale of alternative responses did indeed evoke distributions of sentiment suggesting substantial variation in delegates' images of themselves as independent decision-makers. Using a nominal division between delegates at one extreme or the other and leaving the remainder in the middle, one can distinguish "trustees" from "mandated delegates." In both 1980 and 1984, the modal response clearly favored the role of the trustee who would vote on conscience.

Table 35. Elite Approaches to Decision-Making in Convention

	1980		1984	
Role Preference	Dem.	Rep.	Dem.	Rep.
Vote the way I think is right (trustee)	45%	43%	46%	42
Mixed	34	34	36	36
Vote the way the people I represent would vote (mandated delegate)	21	23	18	22
	100%	100%	100%	100%
Number of cases	795	494	1033	932

See Appendix C for description of the measurement of role preferences.

As Table 35 indicates, the distributions were remarkably alike in both years and across delegates from both parties.

The correlates of these nominal self-classifications in our analyses of similarities and dissimilarities between masses and elites suggest that whether or not representation roles have been articulated for delegates selected to support one or another candidacy, delegates' attitudes reflect their role preferences. Virtually without exception—in both parties, in both years, and on all our measures of political attitudes and preferences— the "trustees' " mean positions accentuated party polarization by being extremely liberal among Democrats and extremely conservative among Republicans. The mean of the intrastate differences between the preferences of elite activists and their rank-and-file constituency were greatest for the trustees and least for the self-designated "mandated representatives," whose attitudes were visibly more moderate than the attitudes of trustees. As a consequence, our correlational measures of similarity and dissimilarity between elites and ordinary citizens, presented in Table 36, reflect substantially higher indicators of dissimilarity for Trustees than for their counterparts who would act as delegates on behalf of their constituents.

It is worth observing that in Table 36 the role-related differences in predispositions, attitudes, and group assessments all pertain to substantive questions quite different from those involved in the context evoking the role differentiations made by the delegates. In neither year were the topics demanding delegate decisions in convention (the focus for our question on roles) a direct reflection of the policy preferences and issue attitudes that formed the basis for our analysis. This is more than suggestive evidence that delegates who differ with regard to their avowed preferences for representational roles differ more generically in their propensity to attend to or ignore the opinions of rank-and-file partisans. In other words, it would seem that we have clear and direct evidence that our political elites are accustomed to articulating their political performance in terms of representational roles, and thus as individuals they take part directly, if not self-consciously, in the representational activity of the conventions.

The general conclusion from the twelve mass-elite comparisons possible in 1984 (Table 36) and the ten comparisons in 1980 is that trustees are less representative of party masses than are elite activists who prefer to behave as instructed if not as mandated delegates. In both years the role-related differences are much sharper among Democratic than Republican activists. The reason for this is not apparent. There is no difference across parties in the incidence of role preferences that might suggest differences in correlates, but in ten of the eleven interparty comparisons from 1980 and 1984, role-related differences in the representativeness of Democratic elites are greater than among Republican elites.

We are now better prepared to understand the one exception. It pertains to the 1984 topic of domestic spending. On the question of governmental spending for domestic programs, the usual pattern of role-related differences was present for Republicans, but in contrast to the usually sharp differences among Democrats, Democratic trustees exhibited slightly greater similarity to the Democratic masses than did instructed

Table 36. Mass-Elite Similarities for Trustees and Mandated Delegates

Elite Role	Liberal Conservative		Social Issues		Foreign Policy		Domestic Spending		New Politics		Traditional Groups	
	Dem.	Rep.	Dem.	Rep.	Dem.	Rep.	Dem.	Rep.	Dem.	Rep.	Dem.	Rep.
1980												
Trustee	.45	−.05	.34	−.35	.40	−.19			.35	−.29	.49	−.56
Mandated/instructed delegates	.15	−.06	.08	−.30	.13	−.12			.10	−.23	.27	−.51
Difference	+.30	−.01	+.26	+.05	+.27	+.07			+.25	+.06	+.22	+.05
1984												
Trustee	.42	−.32	.59	−.15	.45	−.24	.09	−.60	.25	−.32	.41	−.55
Mandated/instructed delegates	.14	−.24	.29	−.06	.27	−.12	.11	−.46	.03	−.27	.21	−.47
Difference	+.28	+.08	+.30	+.09	+.18	+.12	−.02	+.14	+.22	+.05	+.20	+.08

Plus (+) indicates that policy preferences of elites choosing a "mandated delegate" role are *more similar* to those of their party's mass supporters than are the preferences of the self-designated "trustees."

delegates. The differences are small on the correlational measure (.09 to .11 in Table 36), but they are unmistakable on the measure of differences in national means (differences of 2 and 5) or mean differences of state means (3.7 to 4.9). We now know, however, that the more liberal Democratic activists were more like the rank and file on this one topic than were the less liberal Democrats (in contrast to the obverse in all other domains); as a consequence, the more liberal trustees were more similar to the masses than were the more moderate instructed delegates.

The otherwise ubiquitous party differences may be used to add to one of the earlier points of this chapter. Role differences were much more evident among Democratic activists, but it does not seem appropriate to conclude that Democrats who took the role of instructed delegates were more inclined to representational behavior that were their Republican counterparts; as often as not, Democratic instructed delegates were *less* similar to mass Democrats than were Republican instructed delegates to mass Republicans. Nor were Democratic trustees less like their national rank and file than Republican trustees were unlike their supporters. And yet both groups contributed to a pattern in which evidence of representation is more pronounced among Democrats than among Republicans. And so, we have systematic party differences that certainly can be described as associated with greater or lesser representativeness of elites, but should they be described in terms of representation?

Local/National Orientation

The same ambiguity arises in interpreting the empirical consequences of another inquiry in the 1980 and 1984 studies. With an eye to determining something about the parochial/cosmopolitan nature of the presidential selection process—is it national politics or is it local politics on a national scene?—

Table 37. National/Local Orientation of Elites

| | 1980 | | 1984 | |
Orientation	Dem.	Rep.	Dem.	Rep.
National	45%	53%	45%	41%
Mixed	5	5	6	8
Local	50	42	49	51
	100%	100%	100%	100%
Number of cases	826	618	987	902

See Appendix C for an operational definition of the focus of orientation.

we also queried our delegate subjects in both 1980 and 1984 about behaviors that might indicate a difference between more parochial and more cosmopolitan orientations. To put the matter somewhat more prosaically, we asked our respondents to describe the focus of their general political conversations: were they concerned with national issues or with local issues? Their responses are reported in Table 37. In terms of both the substance of the issues under examination and the analytic question of congruence between elite and mass attitudes in their home constituencies, the distinction between national and local orientation proved to be another way of distinguishing greater and lesser interconnectedness between mass and elite policy preferences.

Although our interest in distinguishing the more parochial from the more cosmopolitan was a direct offshoot of our search for indications of local ties binding representatives to the represented, it turned out as an empirical matter that the two indicators of orientation (role and focus of activity) were virtually unrelated. Among activists with a national orientation, trustees outnumbered instructed/mandated delegates 60 to 27; among activists with a local orientation, the ratio was 53 to 31. Whatever difference there was, of course, was in the "expected" direction, the more parochial outlook being that of the instructed delegate and the national orientation slightly more common to the trustee. However, the differences were very slight.

As a consequence, it is of great interest to observe in Table 38 that local/national orientations seem to be almost as effective as are the indicators of role preference in separating out elites whose attitudes are more or less similar to those of rank-and-file partisans. In both parties, elite activists with a national orientation held the more extreme issue positions and therefore accentuated party differences, while their colleagues with a more local orientation were visibly more moderate in their policy commitments. These differences were then associated with larger and smaller differences of means based on state-to-state comparisons of elite and mass attitudes. As can be observed in Table 38, the correlational measures of dissimilarity were generally larger for nationally oriented Democrats and Republicans than for their colleagues who reported a stronger orientation toward local matters.

In a comparison of the 1984 correlational scores of dissimilarity associated with national and local focus for discussions of politics, it is clear that the differences are not as sharp as those associated with differences in activists' representational role preferences. The same distinction could be observed in the 1980 data, although not as sharply there because the national/local contrasts were somewhat greater in the earlier year. These interyear differences may be worthy of future exploration, but for the moment it seems sufficient to conclude that we have identified yet another arena of political behavior that produces significant variation in the representativeness of political elites.

In the present inquiry we have not returned to our original curiosity as to whether national and local orientations make a difference in the subsequent convention or campaign activities of delegates. It seems quite possible that we have captured some part of a distinction that, if more adequately defined and measured, has many implications for the conduct of presiden-

Table 38. Mass-Elite Similarities and Delegate Orientation

Orientation	Liberal/Conservative		Social Issues		Foreign Policy		Domestic Spending		New Politics		Traditional Groups	
	Dem.	Rep.	Dem.	Rep.	Dem.	Rep.	Dem.	Rep.	Dem.	Rep.	Dem.	Rep.
1980												
National	.41	−.12	.31	−.41	.37	−.24			.32	−.36	.46	−.62
Local	.31	−.03	.26	−.25	.29	−.10			.27	−.18	.41	−.50
Difference	+.10	+.09	+.05	+.16	+.03	+.14			+.05	+.18	+.05	+.12
1984												
National	.40	−.35	.49	−.19	.46	−.25	.12	−.58	.20	−.32	.41	−.56
Local	.27	−.20	.50	−.09	.39	−.12	.13	−.53	.16	−.30	.33	−.53
Difference	+.13	+.15	−.01	+.10	+.07	+.13	−.01	+.05	+.04	+.02	+.08	+.03

Plus (+) indicates that policy preferences of elites with a "local orientation" are *more similar* to those of their party's mass supporters than are the preferences of elites with a "national" orientation.

tial politics. Our instrumental use of the information suggests that there is more to be derived from understanding patterns of behavior not self-consciously directed toward elite representational activity.

The inquiry into the representational roles and local or national focus of elite political interests highlights the possibility that our different measures may have different meanings for the explications of "linkage." In both of the analyses just reviewed, the differences of state-based means provided the clearest evidence of the effects of role preference and orientation on mass-elite similarities. The correlations of national distributions and the comparisons of national means supported the same substantive conclusion, but the state-based measures provided by far the sharpest evidence. After the fact, the reason seems intuitively clear.

Both those who prefer to make decisions as instructed delegates and those who normally prefer to talk local politics have implicitly identified mechanisms that could link their attitudes to those of members of the mass population. The "locals," in particular, have identified their "significant others" as other locals. Only one of our three statistics, the national mean of state-based differences in elite and mass means, explicitly links the elite activist to a (more or less) local mass, whether or not it is a constituency to be represented. The other two statistics, the correlational measure of dissimilarity and the mean difference of national groups of individual numbers of the elites and masses, do not rest on any such bond between elite and specified subsets of the mass.

Now if the link creating similarities between elites and masses is interpersonal contact, would it not be better to measure the similarity with a statistic comparing local means? Indeed, unless there is some reason that the total set of elites engaging in interpersonal contact with rank-and-file partisans have systematically different attitudes from those elites who do not contact rank-and-file partisans, there is no reason to expect national statistics comparing each group of elites to the same national population of rank-and-file partisans to reveal any difference. A measure based directly on local differences would seem a more appropriate test of the presumed explanation.

There are, of course, national differences between some groups of elites who are to be compared with a given national partisan mass. Where that is so—as among elites with more extreme policy preferences who campaign on behalf of issues—correlational measures and comparisons of national means are both a proper base for the analysis. In the same situation, states are but microcosms of the nation and, on the average, reveal the same differences when the third measure— the mean of state-based differences of means—is examined.

We are now acutely aware that the match between the geographic location of referents used in the questionnaire and the geographic bases for examining mass-elite similarities is not a strong point of our study design. We have matched elites and masses analytically at the level of the state for purposes of deriving statistics comparing issue or policy preference domains. But in specifying conditions that might affect or constitute linkage, the questionnaire asked about the strength of party organization "in your home community," about party competition at the "most local level," and about "people you talk to" with no anticipation of a subsequent need to match subsets of elites with statewide or districted populations. The possible dividends of such an improvement in the design of future studies is suggested by the extraordinarily large mean differences of state-based elite-mass comparisons in our analysis of local/national orientations. The notable accentuation of state-based differences of means in this specific analysis prompted these comments; we must reserve a systematic inquiry on this topic for future research. At this point we simply note that despite the uniformity with which all three statistics, in both years, support the substantive findings discussed here, there seem to be instances in which the measures of mass-elite similarity differ in a manner that suggests different levels—

micro and macro—for the linkages that create mass-elite similarities.

Delegate Selection

Under the impetus of Democratic party reform, the rules and procedures for delegate selection have undergone almost constant revision since 1968. Much of the commentary, both professional and public, has centered on the rapid expansion of the use of the primary election as a device to democratize delegate selection. This is not the appropriate place for a comprehensive review of the impact of the primaries on partisan politics in the late twentieth century. The diversion would be too great, and it would be complicated by the need to reconcile public accounts with an interesting aspect of our delegates' own reports of how they came to be delegates. For example, although most reports specify that some 75 percent of all 1980 delegates were elected in the 1980 primaries, and 60 percent of the 1984 delegates in 1984 primaries, the delegates' own reports to a somewhat different question are instructive. In both 1980 and 1984, they were asked: "When you were selected as a delegate to the national convention, were you selected as a direct result of a primary? as a direct result of a state or district convention or caucus? by a meeting of other delegates from your state? by a preexisting party committee? or as one of the 'Super Delegates' for public or party positions?"

The intraparty distributions of their answers in each of the two data collections are displayed in Table 39. Apparently only minor fractions—in both parties and both years—agreed with the "official" reports of the incidence of selection by primary election. We have not as yet exhausted our exploration of this striking difference. Our best hunch at this stage, however, is that many delegates in our study saw as the crucial decisions in their selection those that determined whether they would be on a primary election ballot. (Defeated candidates, who are

Table 39. Reported Mode of Delegate Selection

	1980		1984	
	Dem.	Rep.	Dem.	Rep.
Primary	18%	41%	30%	22%
Convention or caucus	65	46	48	49
Other delegates	6	3	7	2
Party committee	4	10	5	22
Super delegates	7	—	10	5
	100%	100%	100%	100%
Number of cases	448	286	618	499

See Appendix C for a description of the categories of delegate selection.

not represented in our study, might well have provided even more reports that they were not delegates because they—or their candidates—were defeated in primary elections.) The responses to our question belie the importance generally assigned to primary elections and emphasize the importance of traditional party organizations in delegate selection. Upon closer inspection, these reports may prove misleading as indicators of the balance of power between party and candidate, but they clearly diminish the status recently accorded the primary election voter.

Before pursuing the representational correlates of the mode of delegate selection, we examined the interaction between mode of selection and reported status as representative. Traditionally, delegates in both parties are formally classified as representing either congressional districts or state constituencies at large. In addition, in both parties there are delegates who, according to their own reports, are chosen because they were elected officials or party officials, but this category was not well represented in our study in either party. On the Democratic side, Super Delegates were notable underrepresented in our sample of elite respondents; Republicans of high formal

Table 40. Delegate Selection by Mode and Status

Elected in Primary	Representing District	1980 Dem.	1980 Rep.	1984 Dem.	1984 Rep.
yes	yes	33%	17%	30%	19%
yes	no	5	2	1	3
no	yes	38	55	38	52
no	no	17	20	23	26
Super delegate		7	4	8	—
		100%	100%	100%	100%
Number of cases		446	284	591	483

position were infrequent participators in our study as well. It is also true that the Republican party has not matched the Democratic party's emphasis on reform and has therefore not felt the same need to create a counter-reformation by giving special emphasis to the representation of their elected leaders. Nevertheless, in our classification of modes of selection, the high-status members from both parties were held out for separate analysis.

Among the remainder it turned out that virtually all delegates chosen in primary elections were chosen to represent districts. Nevertheless, it is most economical and straightforward to present data derived from five categories of delegate selection, represented in national distributions from 1980 and 1984 in Table 40. Among the five, delegates chosen at large by primary election are so few in number as to defy reliable estimates of correlates.

In both 1980 and 1984, patterns of differences in representativeness of elite policy preferences were distinct and three in number. In both years and on virtually all measures, Democratic Super Delegates were clearly the most representative of rank-and-file policy preferences, as reflected in Table 41. This finding is not necessarily a complete surprise—probably no

Table 41. Delegate Selection and Mass-Elite Similarities

Elected in primary	Representing district	Liberal/Conservative		Social Issues		Foreign Policy		Domestic Spending		New Politics		Traditional Groups	
		Dem.	Rep.	Dem.	Rep.	Dem.	Rep.	Dem.	Rep.	Dem.	Rep.	Dem.	Rep.
1980													
yes	yes	.13	−.05	.13	−.29	.16	−.14			.18	−.27	.32	−.45
yes	no	—	—	—	—	—	—			—	—	—	—
no	yes	.30	−.05	.25	−.31	.27	−.17			.28	−.29	.45	−.47
no	no	.26	−.03	.21	−.22	.23	−.09			.29	−.18	.40	−.36
Super Delegate		.10		.11		.15				.14		.22	
1984													
yes	yes	.27	−.14	.46	−.11	.34	−.08	−.08	−.38	.14	−.24	.29	−.33
yes	no	—	—	—	—	—	—	—	—	—	—	—	—
no	yes	.29	−.32	.46	−.20	.37	−.26	−.12	−.53	.11	−.34	.35	−.54
no	no	.29	−.17	.55	.01	.32	−.11	.00	−.45	.17	−.21	.30	−.41
Super Delegate		.12		.38		.21		−.13		.09		.20	

No entry is shown where the number of elite cases is less than 25.

surprise at all to the defenders of party as a crucial political institution. There is, nevertheless, a nice irony in the fact that Super Delegates were added to the Democratic convention to counter the populist anti-party influences presumably introduced by expanding the number of primary elections. The evidence of close rapport between rank-and-file partisans and Democratic party and public officials is striking on all three of our measures of representativeness. The correlational assessments show relatively greater similarity between the national distributions of sentiments in both years. Elected officials, party and public, reflect public policy sentiments, whether or not they also reflect informal judgments as to the candidates best suited to produce party victory in November. The Super Delegates may have given the traditional wielders of power more representation in the selection of the nominees, but they also inadvertently outdid the primary election winners in representing public opinion.

As Table 41 illustrates, the irony is compounded by evidence that delegates elected in primaries are second only to elected officials in being in tune with given public sentiments. Compared to delegates chosen by the traditional party mechanisms of convention or caucus, delegates chosen by primary election are more representative of the party's rank and file—just as the advocates of primary elections hoped they would be. Irony exists, of course, only in the context of reforms enacted in the name of facilitating or inhibiting particular candidacies. Presumably, Super Delegates were proposed to reestablish the control of the professional politicians over the adventurism of ideological, candidate-inspired amateurs—this in reaction to the anti-party spirit that initiated the reforms to increase access and broaden participation in the presidential selection process.

Whether or not the goals of party protectors or candidacy advocates were served we cannot tell. Our only criterion concerns the representation of mass sentiment on matters of policy and issue preference. It seems apparent that the initial goal of the reforms was to advance causes that were demonstrably *not* mainstream, rank-and-file goals. The established officialdom, in turn, may have feared the unchanneled voices of the masses in primaries—or may have been concerned only with the promotion of viable and electable candidates. Our singular preoccupation with the representation of mass sentiments does not equip us to test the extent to which the process has met other goals as it has been reshaped. We can simply note that delegates elected in primaries are not themselves ideological extremists. Compared to delegates selected by other processes—including conventions, party caucuses, and meetings of other elites— delegates selected by primary election are relatively in tune with the centrist preferences of the rank and file. We can also repeat that whether or not the Super Delegates are better equipped to make wise and prudent nominations against the popular will, they themselves are the most efficient representatives of that will as expressed in policy and issue preferences.

The third distinctive pattern visible in Table 41 is that delegates chosen by convention or caucus to represent congressional district infrastructures turn out to be the least representative of public sentiments. Most interesting is the extent to which the difference between the role as district representative and the role of delegate at large is consistently associated with differences in the representativeness of the delegates. In both years, in both parties, and in most substantive domains, delegates chosen by caucus or convention to be representatives at large are more representative of rank-and-file citizen sentiments than are the delegates chosen to represent the interests of a congressional district.

The pattern suggests limited and parochial perspectives on the part of those controlling delegate selection at the district level. Mean scores are neither at the ideological extremes of those chosen at large nor the moderate scores of the Super Delegates. They simply seem out of line with whatever rank-and-file comparison is examined. The preservation of local control does not appear to have facilitated or enhanced the representation of rank-and-file policy preferences.

8

Individuals, Institutions, and Representation

Very few of the thousands of people, from ordinary citizens to extraordinary leaders, whose attitudes and actions have been reported in this book engage in politics as anything more than a part-time, spare-time avocation. Except for the handful of officeholders who are dependent on political office—public or party—for their livelihood, political participation is a completely voluntary activity. As such, it attracts people with a thousand and one different motives for becoming engaged. To judge from motives for participation reported in studies of political activists, a concern with governmental representation of popular issue preferences is not high on the list. Nevertheless, we have found an extended variety of circumstances under which voluntary political activists with policy preferences more and less representative of mass preferences can be identified.

The results of the analyses reported here are evidence of the existence of institutions that make the process of presidential selection something more than an atomistic personal or even partisan popularity contest. The "political system," including many aspects not mentioned in the foregoing discussion, quite apparently produces a representation of public policy preferences even where the formal rules and overt activities of the participants are not designed primarily for such purposes. The political analyst's usual concern with representation centers on the legislative process, where the ultimate enactment of policy that responds to popular demand is one of the normative tests of the entire democratic system. There, all manner of institutions—for example, frequent regular elections, in single-member districts, of persons to represent contiguous constituencies—have been created in the name of the consent of the governed and the accountability of those elected to govern. Not so for the selection of delegates to the national nominating convention: that process stands in sharp contrast, devoid of any direct procedures concerned with the responsibility of the delegates to anyone other than a candidate for nomination.

In the process of presidential selection the political party is the principal institution responsible for bringing order out of what would otherwise be the chaos of voluntary political action. The party does not exist in order to provide an entity that is responsible to the citizenry for obtaining consent and providing accountability; nevertheless, it performs equivalent functions. In a very real sense, party defines orthodoxy of political belief and legitimacy of political action. Parties are slow to impose sanctions on the heterodox, and they are sometimes very slow to adapt the definition of the party line to fit changing times. By the same token, much of the continuity in the content of national political controversy comes from the continuity provided by partisan ideology.

Taken as an absolute standard, the party line may inhibit would-be leaders in their attempts to be responsive to public opinion. But compared with other sources of guidance on issues of public policy, party functions to link leaders to their base of mass support. Candidacies for the presidency, if not candidates themselves, derive some of their distinctiveness from their deviations from the party line, and those activists who are motivated by the distinctive appeal of one candidate over another appear to be less responsive to the existing opinions of their fellow partisans in the electorate at large than are the activists who consciously attempt to represent party interests. The candidate who tries to represent the purity of ideological conviction or, more simply, commitment to a specific policy outcome from government stands as the virtual antithesis to the representative of party, at least where the representative nature of policy preferences is concerned. Party as the mobilizer of activists, the guide for activists' decisions, the shaper of the local context for activists' participation, or the goal for activists' efforts does more than candidate loyalty or ideological conviction to preserve the bond between the leaders and the led.

The very certainty of this conclusion points to a major limitation of the present inquiry into mass-elite linkages. Precisely because virtually all our findings have been presented in replicate for two electoral contexts, 1980 and 1984, we are as devoid of new insights into the nature of political change as we are confident of our increased knowledge about political continuity. Political leadership would seem to be the essential source of political change, but we have been limited in our ability to point to evidence that this is so. Indeed, we note the election and reelection of Reagan in the face of an ideological stance among his elite supporters that had them persistently at odds with the Republican rank and file, to say nothing of the Democrats from which he drew vital electoral support. And neither the greater representativeness of the relatively moderate Mondale supporters nor the centrism of the Carter campaign elite saved their candidates from massive popular rejection. Moreover, we have found that elite activists representing or promoting specific issues are among those least representative of public opinion.

However, the period covered by our inquiry did not witness any discernible change of mass opinions that appeared responsive to elite initiatives. In the comparable but less than identical measures of similarities of mass and elite policy preferences in 1980 and 1984 there is little evidence of increased mass-elite rapport within either party. Indeed, among Republicans, as we noted in Chapter 3, there is marginal evidence of a widened gap between elite and mass opinion. This may have occurred because mass opinion lagged behind in its response to the new conservatism of 1980, or it may have been the result of the actual failure of the Republican elite to lead

their mass followers as they themselves shifted their preferences to the left between 1980 and 1984.

The basic obstacle to our learning more about the dynamics
of mass-elite interaction that produces change lies in the relative absence of changes in mass opinion during the period under
investigation. One major contribution of the present discussion,
therefore (and of that previously presented in *Parties in Transition*), may well be the recasting of the problem of opinion
leadership as a problem in reducing tensions induced by dissimilarities in mass-elite policy preferences. Such a recasting,
in turn, may consist of emphasizing the structural facilitation
of change through the circulation of the elites, through the
modes of delegate selection, or through the engagement of any
of the structures or institutions that we have identified as providing better, or at least more, mass-elite linkage.

An interest in the study of political change exposes another
limitation of the present investigation. Although we have now
identified a series of circumstances or conditions associated
with greater or lesser similarity in mass and elite policy preferences, we have not significantly contributed to better specification of the precise mechanisms that produce the variations
in linkage. For example, we are satisfied that an electoral context defined by close *inter*party competition is associated with
tighter *intra*party linkage of mass and elite policy preferences,
but none of our evidence offers explicit explanation for the
phenomenon. Does the threat of loss to the other party induce
a conservative effort by partisan elites to ensure retention of
their own natural partisan base? Or does something more related to a culture of competitiveness induce moderation in their
outlook?

An even more perplexing example is provided by the assessment of role preferences. Granted a generalized desire to
do as those you represent desire, how does the elite activist's
preference for the role of instructed or mandated delegate work
to enhance the extent to which his or her policy preferences
match those of the party's electoral base? Is the answer to be

found in the reshaping of the activist's own preferences? What is the mechanism or device that produces enough information—the cognitive input—to make the efforts to be representative actually produce great representativeness? This question is particularly perplexing when representativeness is measured as a matter of similarities of national distributions, not just special relationships with home constituencies.

In like manner, we have found that a local orientation on the part of elites produces closer mass-elite linkage than does a more national perspective. How does this come about? In one of the few instances in which we attempted to test an explanatory hypothesis, our intuitive logic failed us. Employing a 1984 question about the amount of activity in state and local party politics, we hypothesized that a high level of local activity would have the same meaning as a local orientation in providing the explanation of mass-elite similarities in issue preferences. This was not the case. Chapter 7 did not include elite state and local activity as one of the components of specification precisely because of the *absence* of evidence that it made any systematic difference to mass-elite similarities of issue preference. Therefore, neither the interpersonal contact nor the psychological engagement that such activity might imply can be used to explain the clear and predictable evidence that local orientations—or instructed delegate roles, for that matter—are associated with tighter mass-elite linkages.

Although less perplexing, the data pertaining to the mode of delegate selection also need further explication. If primary elections do enhance mass-elite similarities in issue preferences, and if caucus or convention selection to represent the congressional district minimizes such similarities, how does this happen? Is it the voters' choices that select the delegate candidates with congruent preferences? Are those who select potential delegates as representatives of the state at large somehow more public-minded than those who select delegates to represent the more localized home district? And are Super Delegates closely linked to mass opinion because of the moderation of their own preferences, or is there something about their status or background and experience that makes them such good representatives?

Without elaborating further examples, it is possible to enunciate a general point: evidence that certain institutions or legal constraints or psychological perspectives are associated with greater or lesser degrees of similarity in mass and elite policy preferences generally identifies a new puzzle—how do we now specify the particular psychological or behavioral mechanisms that make the difference? It is not difficult to conjure up hypotheses to account for much that we have observed. The task of this book has been to identify the institutions that channel and organize the volunteered activities of elite activists into patterns that look like the results of a system or the intended outcomes of a deliberately designed process. One of the unfinished tasks is to seek the *next* level of explanation.

A portion of the waiting research agenda can be addressed with the evidence at hand. The analysis in this effort has been largely at the conceptual level of bivariate explorations. Granted, we have dealt simultaneously with a multiplicity of indicators of policy preferences, among two populations of actors—elite and mass—in each of two parties and in two very different electoral settings. These complexities aside, the basic analytic mode has been to examine the impact of independent variables, one variable at a time, on one mass-elite relationship—and then to replicate that analysis.

Upon rare occasion we have made a simple check on possible confounding interpretations and have found, for example, that national/local differences in orientation are only mildly associated with trustee/delegate differences in role preference. We were also prepared to juxtapose variations associated with different candidates' support groups and variations associated with institutional differences. We then discovered institutional differences associated with different candidacies, but in most instances the introduction of candidate preference differences into analyses of institutional differences provided simply one more instance of replicated findings.

Despite these occasional forays into more complex analytic models, we have not pretended to exhaust the possibilities inherent in the data collections employed in the present study. Moreover, both of the elite data collections contain a rich battery of biographical information on individuals' political careers in seeking, holding, and aspiring to both public and party office. Despite the likelihood that the experiences and expectations embedded in such records have real consequences for the representativeness of policy preferences, limitations on our resources—including time—have left this domain totally unexplored.

Yet another challenge for the future pertains to problems of measurement. We pursued alternative modes of measuring the similarity of mass and elite policy preferences far enough to be persuaded that three of four measures produced analyses that called for, or supported, virtually identical interpretations at our level of exploratory description. As noted earlier, we rejected the measure of dyadic correlations because of its apparent instability. Yet it was the ingredients of that fourth measure—state-level estimates of means for elite subgroups and for rank-and-file partisans—that were used to create the third measure: the mean differences of state means, which produced results that matched the other two acceptable measures.

We relied on the differences in national distributions of individual-level data for illustrating most of our conclusions. One measure reflected differences of national means; the other was based on the correlation between issue preferences and group (mass-elite) differences. The match between them was very close with a very high correlation—but also a steep slope, reflecting the fact that there was much greater variance in the correlations than in the difference of means. As a consequence, we made most use of the collective correlations because of the greater clarity with which they reflected analytic differences.

We were surprised that the attempt to use state-based estimates was not more fruitful. Given the generally limited interstate variance of many of the measures of mass opinion, we were not surprised that the dyadic correlations proved to be quite unstable; however, we had anticipated systematic differences on the occasions when state-based means should accentuate differences also observed in the comparisons of national distributions. For example, it seemed likely that delegates from areas with strong party organizations would resemble their state constituencies even more than they resembled their party's national mass constituency. Yet this seemed not to be so. These and other ambiguities in the meaning to be attached to alternative measurements must be resolved as a part of the effort to provide evidence specifying the mechanisms that produce the results we have observed.

This monograph is virtually unique as an examination of essentially political factors that influence mass-elite linkages in matters of policy preference. The uniqueness lies more in the fact that two data collections were carried out to support the investigation than in the substantive details of the study design. As the plans for the studies—the 1984 study in particular—were developed, we simply constructed a questionnaire containing content of obvious interest to a host of political analysts, observers, and participants. It is perhaps a comment on the utility of such conventional wisdom that virtually all the "obvious" questions we asked bore fruit. Of course, we would have been bewildered if trustees had not differed from instructed delegates in the faithfulness with which they represented public opinion. Now that we "know" they do, we must explain how this is possible in national populations of representers and represented who are voluntarily engaged in a process structured by political institutions that are not intended to do more than choose the most electable candidate for president.

Both the design of the studies and the execution of the analyses reflect our commitment to learn more about how our political system works. As a practical matter, better information and more complete understanding of mass-elite linkages will be useful in guiding future efforts at the reform and redesign of our electoral institutions. The recent history of political reform has been marked more by ideological conviction than by expert understanding of the institutional forms being amended. As a consequence, the electoral process has been plagued with the unanticipated consequences of ill-considered changes. Inquiries such as this one move us forward in identifying the institutions, be they matters of legal prescription or behavioral custom, that are relevant to particular outcomes. A more thorough comprehension of the specific mechanisms responsible for institutional consequences will presumably make the results of future reforms a bit more predictable and, therefore, more effective.

A second and more profound purpose is also served by the present study: it permits fuller appreciation of our system of government and thereby enhances our commitment to its norms and objectives. In an age of cynicism it is important to have evidence that the system works. Our research has adduced evidence that institutional forms related to delegate recruitment and role preferences, delegate perspectives related to local politics and regard for party, electoral competition, and the party itself all make a difference in the enhancement or inhibition of mass-elite linkages. We have not learned enough to make normative judgments about how much linkage is ideal for what purposes nor, at this stage, how best to alter a given degree of linkage. Nevertheless, more such studies will both enrich our understanding of the political system and influence the ways in which we try to sustain or change institutions in order to realize our normative commitments to democratic politics.

Appendix A. Data Sources

The basic design for analysis compares attributes of a partisan group of elite activists with the same attributes exhibited by ordinary citizens—voters and nonvoters alike—who constitute their partisan supporters in the electorate. The mass electorate was represented by national samples selected by the National Election Studies data collections in 1980 and 1984. The partisan groups within the electorate were identified through their responses to the standard NES question on party identification: "Generally speaking, do you usually think of yourself as a Republican, a Democratic, an Independent, or what?" Those respondents initially selecting Republican or Democrat were then asked: "Would you call yourself a strong [party name] or not a very strong [party name]?" This yielded four categories. Those replying "Independent" (or volunteering other or no preference) were asked: "Do you think of yourself as closer to the Republican or Democratic party?" Those picking one of the parties were classified as Independent leaners, thus yielding two more categories. Those not selecting a party constituted the residual seventh group of Independents. "Apoliticals" have been dropped from this analysis.

Each partisan group included all who identified with one party, whether that identification was strong or weak, plus all non-identifiers who expressed a preference for that party. In general, therefore, independents and other nonpartisans—approximately 10 percent of the electorate—were excluded from the analyses. The partisan groups in the electorate are variously referred to as "rank-and-file supporters," "mass supporters," "mass partisans," "ordinary citizens," and at times "the voters," even though nonvoters are always included in estimates of mass partisan attributes.

The elite activists are represented by those delegates to the national nominating conventions of 1980 and 1984 who returned mail questionnaires (sent out to the complete population of delegates) *and* who reported participating in the presidential election campaign of either year. Their patterns of delegateship and participation are reported in Table 15 (Chapter 3).

In both 1973 and 1981 a major effort was devoted to analyzing the mail questionnaire respondents for their representativeness of the universe of all delegates. Those efforts are reported at length in Jeane Kirkpatrick, *The New Presidential Elite*, and, more pertinently, in Warren E. Miller and M. Kent Jennings, *Parties in Transition*. The clear evidence that mail respondents were not a biased subset of the universe of delegate activists of those years led us to undertake a 1985 data collection following the 1984 election.

The analysis of respondents following the 1980 election rested in large part on comparisons of data from those "panel" respondents who participated in both the 1972 and 1980 studies. In similar fashion, the 1985 respondents included many who had been respondents in 1981 and for whom comparisons of 1981 and 1985 data could be made. The 1985 data collection used the same methods and procedures as those used in 1981, and we have seen no reason to be less satisfied with the quality and representativeness of the resulting file of 1984 information than with the data from the 1972 and 1980 studies.

The data underlying our decision not to report dyadic correlations as measures of mass-elite similarities are reviewed here not as a comment on the representativeness of the data collection but in the interest of explicating a measurement decision directly relevant to the representativeness of mass-elite comparisons. Since dyadic correlations rest on establishing the thirty states represented in the NES sample as the units of analysis, it is worth noting that a laborious reweighting of the 1980 data was carried out in order to correct for over- or underrepresentation of partisan groups in individual states. The results of that effort found no bias relevant to the representation of states, and we do not believe the erratic patterns of dyadic correlations observed in explorations of the 1984 data can be traced to problems involved in the representation of states in our NES sample design. It is true that exclusive reliance on the NES designation of sample states would have eliminated elites of the other twenty states from our inter-elite analyses (comparing marginal distributions of different elite groups), but the decision to forgo reliance on the NES sample (as providing proper representation of state populations)

Table A1. Eta Values Associated with Six Variables and Four
Groups

Policy Domains	Democrats		Republicans	
	Mass	Elite	Mass	Elite
Liberal/conservative	.09	.06	.09	.26
Social issues	.13	.08	.18	.17
Foreign policy	.14	.03	.07	.23
Spending	.11	.05	.16	.16
New Politics	.15	.06	.08	.10
Traditional groups	.16	.10	.11	.27

Eta is a measure of the ratio of variances among states to the variances within states. Smaller entries indicate limited variation among states compared to within-state variation, and therefore suggest greater instability of correlations based on state means.

stemmed only from the apparently limited interstate variance on our crucial dependent variables.

Table A1 indicates low values for the eta statistic, calculated to reflect the relationship between interstate variance and intrastate variance. Although two or three estimates for the Republican elite approach levels that might indicate stability for correlations based on interstate variability, eta's for the Republican mass partisans and both groups of Democrats were so low that we rejected that option for our measurement of mass-elite similarities.

Finally, the data used in defining the parties' leadership wings are presented in Table A2. Factor analyses defining leadership wings: rotated factor matrix from a Varimax Rotation using Kaiser's Normalization.

Table A2. Data Base for Party Leadership Wings

	Factor 1	Factor 2	Factor 3
	DEMOCRATS		
Carter	.60	.15	.15
Humphrey	.81	.14	.03
Johnson	.75	−.04	.11
Mondale	.73	.40	−.17
Ferraro	.47	.60	.07
Kennedy, E.	.29	.70	.01
Jackson, J.	.06	.73	.16
McGovern	.07	.83	−.01
Glenn	.32	−.18	.73
Hart	−.15	.43	.76
Kennedy, J.F.	.43	.35	.31
Stevenson	.32	.28	.22
	REPUBLICANS		
Goldwater	.74	−.01	
Kemp	.78	−.21	
Nixon	.59	.24	
Reagan	.83	.13	
Bush	.09	.76	
Dole	.00	.68	
Eisenhower	.16	.72	
Ford	−.08	.73	

Entries are factor loadings.

Appendix B. Measures of Policy Preferences

The following dependent variables were examined.

I. Ideological Self-placement

   A. Elite Samples

      For both *1980* and *1984* the question was worded as follows:
      "We hear a lot of talk these days about liberals and conservatives. Here is a seven-point scale on which the political views that people might hold are arranged from extremely liberal [1] to extremely conservative [7]. Where would you place yourself on this scale?" In 1980 the missing data value was 9; in 1984, 8, 9.

   B. Mass Samples

      For both *1980* and *1984* the question was worded as follows:
      "We hear a lot of talk these days about liberals and conservatives. Here is a seven-point scale on which political views that people hold are arranged from extremely liberal [1] to extremely conservative [7]. Where would you place yourself on this scale, or haven't you thought much about this?" The missing data value in both years was 9.

      For the purpose of standardization with other dependent variables, the response values for both questions were transformed from 1 through 7 to 0 through 100: the most extreme liberal response became 0; the most conservative response became 100; and the midpoint, 4, became 50.

II. Domestic Social Issues Index

   A. Elite Samples

      In *1980* this index was constructed from three items:

      1. Busing. "There is much discussion about the best way to deal with racial problems. Some people think letting

children go to their neighborhood schools is so important that they oppose busing. Others think achieving racial integration of schools is so important that it justifies busing children to schools out of their own neighborhoods. Where would you place yourself on the following [7-point] scale?"

1   keeping children in neighborhood schools
7   busing to achieve integration
9   missing data

Scores on this item were recoded to reflect ideological dimensions as follows:

0 = liberal response (5, 6, 7)
1 = moderate response (4)
2 = conservative response (1, 2, 3)

2. Abortion. "There has been much discussion about abortion during recent years. Which one of the opinions listed below best agrees with your view?"

1   Abortion should never be permitted.
2   Abortion should be permitted only if the life and health of the woman are in danger.
3   Abortion should be permitted if, due to personal reasons, the woman would have difficulty in caring for the child.
4   Abortion should never be forbidden.
9   missing data

Scores on this item were recoded to reflect ideological dimensions as follows:

0 = liberal response (4)
1 = moderate reponses (2, 3)
2 = conservative response (1)

3. ERA. "Do you approve or disapprove of the proposed Equal Rights Amendment to the Constitution, sometimes called the ERA amendment?"

1   approve strongly
2   approve somewhat
3   disapprove somewhat
4   disapprove strongly
9   missing data

Scores on this item were recoded to reflect ideological dimensions as follows:

0 = liberal response (1)
1 = moderate reponses (2, 3)
2 = conservative response (4)

The index was constructed by adding the three items together and then recoding the 0 through 6 range of scores to 0 through 100: 0 equals the most liberal, 100 the most conservative score.

In *1984* the domestic social index was constructed from four items:

1. Busing. The wording of the question and recoding of responses were the same as in 1980 (8, 9, missing data).
2. Abortion. The wording of this question and recoding of responses were the same as in 1980 (8, 9, missing data).
3. School Prayer. "Some people think it is all right for the public schools to start each day with a prayer. Others feel that religion does not belong in the public schools but should be taken care of by the family and the church. Which do you think?"

   1   Schools should be allowed to start each day with a prayer.
   2   Schools should be allowed to start each day with a prayer, provided the prayer is silent.
   3   Religion does not belong in the schools.
   8, 9 missing data

   Scores on this item were recoded to reflect ideological dimensions as follows:
   0 = liberal response (3)
   1 = moderate response (2)
   2 = conservative response (1)

4. Aid to Women. "Some people feel that the government in Washington should make every effort to improve the social and economic position of women. Others feel that the government should not make any special effort to help women because they should help themselves. Where would you place yourself on this scale?"

   1   Government should help women.
   7   Women should help themselves.

8, 9 missing data

Scores on this item were recoded to reflect ideological
dimensions as follows:

0 = liberal response (1, 2, 3)
1 = moderate response (4)
2 = conservative response (5, 6, 7)

The index was constructed by adding the four items together
and then recoding the 0 through 8 range of scores to 0 through
100: 0 equals the most liberal, 100: the most conservative
score.

B. Mass Samples

In *1980* this index was constructed from three items:

1. Busing. "There is much discussion about the best way
   to deal with racial problems. Some people think achieving racial integration of schools is so important that it
   justifies busing children to schools out of their own neighborhoods. Others think letting children go to their own
   neighborhood schools is so important that they oppose
   busing. Where would you place yourself on this scale,
   or haven't you thought much about this?"

   1   bus to achieve integration
   7   keep children in neighborhood schools
   0   haven't thought much
   8   don't know
   9   missing data

   Scores on this item were recoded to reflect ideological
   dimensions as follows:

   0 = liberal response (1, 2, 3)
   1 = moderate response (4, 8, 0)
   2 = conservative response (5, 6, 7)

2. Abortion. "There has been some discussion about abortion during recent years. Which one of the opinions on
   this page best agrees with your view? You can just tell
   me the number of the opinion you choose."

   1   By law, abortion should never be permitted.
   2   The law should permit abortion only in case of
        rape, incest, or when a woman's life is in danger.
   3   The law should permit abortion for reasons other
        than rape, incest, or danger to the woman's life,

but only after the need for the abortion has been
clearly established.

4   By law, a woman should always be able to obtain
     an abortion as a matter of personal choice.

8   don't know

9   missing data

Scores on this item were recoded to reflect ideological
dimensions as follows:

0 = liberal response (4)

1 = moderate response (2, 3, 8)

2 = conservative response (1)

3. Equal Role for Women. "Recently there has been a lot
   of talk about women's rights. Some people feel that
   women should have an equal role with men in running
   business, industry, and government. Others feel that
   women's place is in the home.
   Where would you place yourself on this scale, or haven't
   you thought much about this?"

   1   equal role

   7   women's place is in home

   0   haven't thought much

   8   don't know

   9   missing data

   Scores on this item were recoded to reflect ideological
   dimensions as follows:

   0 = liberal response (1, 2, 3)

   1 = moderate response (4, 8, 0)

   2 = conservative response (5, 6, 7)

The index was constructed by adding the three items together
and then recoding the 0 through 6 range of scores to 0 through
100: 0 equals the most liberal, 100 the most conservative
score.

In *1984* this index was constructed from four items:

1. Busing. The wording of this question and recoding of
   responses were the same as in 1980.

2. Abortion. The wording of this question and recoding of
   responses were the same as in 1980 (7, 9, missing data).

3. Prayer in school. This variable was created from the
   following two parts:

   a. "Some people think it is all right for the public

schools to start each day with a prayer. Others feel that religion does not belong in the public schools but should be taken care of by the family and the church. Have you been interested enough in this to favor one side over the other?"

1   yes
5   no
8   don't know
9   missing data

b. "Which do you think—schools should be allowed to start each day with a prayer or religion does not belong in the schools?"

1   Schools should be allowed to start each day with a prayer.
5   Religion does not belong in the schools.
7   other; depends
8   don't know
9   missing data

Ideological dimensions were constructed as follows:
0 = liberal response if item 3b above equals 5.
1 = moderate response if 3a equals 5 or 3b equals 7 or 8.
2 = conservative response if 3b equals 1.

4. Aid to Women. "Some people feel that the government in Washington should make every effort to improve the social and economic position of women. Others feel that the government should not make any special effort to help women because they should help themselves. Where would you place yourself on this scale, or haven't you thought much about this?"

1   Government should help women.
7   Women should help themselves.
8   don't know
0   haven't thought much
9   missing data

Scores on this item were recoded to reflect ideological dimensions as follows:
0 = liberal response (1, 2, 3)
1 = moderate response (4, 8, 0)
2 = conservative response (5, 6, 7)

The index was constructed by adding the four items together
and then recoding the 0 through 8 range of scores to 0 through
100: 0 equals the most liberal, 100 the most conservative
score.

III. Foreign Policy and Defense Index
   A. Elite Samples
      In *1980* this index was constructed from two items:
      1. Defense. "Some people believe that we should spend
         much more money for defense. Suppose these people are
         at one end of the scale at point number '1.' Others feel
         that defense spending should be greatly decreased. Sup-
         pose these people are at the other end, at point '7.' And,
         of course, some other people have opinions somewhere
         in between. Where would you place yourself on this
         scale?" The missing data value was 9."
         Scores on this item were recoded to reflect ideological
         dimensions as follows:
         0 = liberal response (5, 6, 7)
         1 = moderate response (4)
         2 = conservative response (1, 2, 3)
      2. Detente. "Some people feel it is important for us to try
         very hard to get along with Russia. Others feel it is a big
         mistake to try too hard to get along with Russia. Where
         would you place yourself on this seven-point scale?"
         1   important to try very hard to get along with Russia
         7   big mistake to try very hard to get along with Rus-
               sia
         9   missing data
         Scores on this item were recoded to reflect ideological
         dimensions as follows:
         0 = liberal response (1, 2, 3)
         1 = moderate response (4)
         2 = conservative response (5, 6, 7)
      The index was constructed by adding the two items to-
      gether and then recoding the 0 through 4 range of scores
      to 0 through 100: 0 equals the most liberal, 100 the most
      conservative score.
      In *1984* this index was constructed from three items:

1. Defense. "Some people believe that we should spend much more money for defense. Others feel that defense spending should be greatly decreased. And, of course, some other people have opinions somewhere in between. Where would you place yourself on this scale?"

1   greatly increase defense spending

7   greatly decrease defense spending

8, 9   missing data

Scores on this item were recoded to reflect ideological dimensions as follows:

0 = liberal response (5, 6, 7)

1 = moderate response (4)

2 = conservative response (1, 2, 3)

2. Detente. The wording of this question and recoding of responses were the same as in 1980 (8, 9, missing data).

3. Central America. "Some people think that the United States should become much more involved in the internal affairs of Central American countries. Others believe that the U.S. should become less involved in this area. Where would you place yourself on this scale?

1   U.S. should become much more involved in Central America.

7   U.S. should become much less involved in Central America.

8, 9   missing data

Scores on this item were recoded to reflect ideological dimensions as follows:

0 = liberal response (5, 6, 7)

1 = moderate response (4)

2 = conservative response (1, 2, 3)

The index was constructed by adding the three items together and then recoding the 0 through 6 range of scores to 0 through 100: 0 equals the most liberal, 100 the most conservative score.

B. Mass Samples

In *1980* this index was created from two items:

1. Defense. "Some people believe that we should spend much less money for defense. Others feel defense spending should be greatly increased. Where would you place

yourself on this scale, or haven't you thought much about
this?"

1   greatly decrease defense spending
7   greatly increase defense spending
0   haven't thought much about this
8   don't know
9   missing data

Scores on this item were recoded to reflect ideological
dimensions as follows:

0 = liberal response (1, 2, 3)
1 = moderate response (0, 4, 8)
2 = conservative response (5, 6, 7)

2. Detente. "Some people feel it is important for us to try
   very hard to get along with Russia. Others feel it is a big
   mistake to try too hard to get along with Russia. Where
   would you place yourself on this scale, or haven't you
   thought much about this?"

   1   important to try very hard to get along with Russia
   7   big mistake to try too hard to get along with Russia
   0   haven't thought much
   8   don't know
   9   missing data

   Scores on this item were recoded to reflect ideological
   dimensions as follows:

   0 = liberal response (1, 2, 3)
   1 = moderate response (0, 4, 8)
   2 = conservative response (5, 6, 7)

The index was constructed by adding the two items together and then recoding the 0 through 4 range of scores
to 0 through 100: 0 equals the most liberal, 100 the most
conservative score.

In *1984* this index was constructed from three items:

1. Defense. The wording of this question and recoding of
   responses were the same as in 1980.

2. Detente. "Some people feel it is important for us to try
   to cooperate more with Russia, while others believe we
   should be much tougher in our dealings with Russia.
   Where would you place yourself on this scale, or haven't
   you thought much about this?"

1   try to cooperate more with Russia
7   get much tougher with Russia
8   don't know
0   haven't thought much
9   missing data
Scores on this item were recoded in the same manner as the 1980 version.
3. Central America. "Some people think that the United States should become much more involved in the internal affairs of Central American countries. Others believe that the U.S. should become less involved in this area. Where would you place yourself on this scale, or haven't you thought much about this?
1   U.S. should become much more involved in Central America.
7   U.S. should become much less involved in central America.
8   I don't know
0   haven't thought much
9   missing data
Scores on this item were recoded to reflect ideological dimensions as follows:
0 = liberal response (5, 6, 7)
1 = moderate response (4, 8, 0)
2 = conservative response (1, 2, 3)
The index was constructed by adding the three items together and then recoding the 0 through 6 range of scores to 0 through 100: 0 equals the most liberal, 100 the most conservative score.

IV. Domestic Spending Index
    A. Elite Samples
       In *1980* there were no items from which to construct this index.
       In *1984* this index was constructed from six items within one question:
       "Listed below are some programs that the federal government currently funds. If you had a say in making up the federal budget this year, indicate for each of the following

programs whether you think federal spending should be increased, reduced, or kept at the same level."

a	dealing with crime	1 = decrease	
b	aid to education	2 = same	
c	medicare	3 = increase	
d	science and technology	8, 9 = missing data	
e	assistance to minorities		
f	social security		

Scores on this item were recoded to reflect ideological dimensions as follows:

0 = liberal response (3)
1 = moderate response (2)
2 = conservative response (1)

The index was constructed by adding the six items together and then recoding the 0 through 12 range of scores to 0 through 100. 0 equals the most liberal score; 100 equals the most conservative score.

B. Mass Samples

This index was not created for 1980.

In *1984* this index was constructed from six items:

"If you had a say in making up the federal budget this year, which programs would you like to see increased and reduced?"

1. "Should federal spending on dealing with crime be increased, decreased, or kept about the same?"

   1 = increased
   2 = same
   3 = decreased
   8 = don't know
   9 = missing data

2. "Should federal spending on schools be increased, decreased, or kept about the same?"

   1 = increased
   2 = same
   3 = decreased
   8 = don't know
   9 = missing data

3. "Should federal spending on Social Security be increased, decreased, or kept about the same?"

       1 = increased
       2 = same
       3 = decreased
       8 = don't know
       9 = missing data

4. "Should federal spending on Medicare be increased, decreased, or kept about the same?"
       1 = increased
       2 = same
       3 = decreased
       8 = don't know
       9 = missing data

5. "Should federal spending on science be increased, decreased, or kept about the same?"
       1 = increased
       2 = same
       3 = decreased
       8 = don't know
       9 = missing data

6. "Should federal spending on aid to minorities be increased, decreased, or kept about the same?"
       1 = increased
       2 = same
       3 = decreased
       8 = don't know
       9 = missing data

Scores on all of the six items were recoded to reflect ideological dimensions as follows:
       0 = liberal response (1)
       1 = moderate response (2, 8)
       2 = conservative response (3)

The index was constructed by adding the six items together and then recoding the 0 through 12 range of scores to 0 through 100: 0 equals the most liberal, 100 the most conservative score.

V. Social Issue Groups Index
  A. Elite Samples
    In *1980* this index was constructed from three feeling ther-

mometers with possible responses ranging from 00 (unfavorable) to 100 (favorable).

"For each of the following groups please indicate your feeling toward them on what we call a 'feeling thermometer.' Here's how it works: If you don't feel either particularly warm or cold toward a group, then you should place them in the middle of the thermometer, at the 50-degree mark. If you have a warm feeling toward a group, or feel favorably toward them, you would give them a score somewhere between 50 degrees and 100 degrees, depending on how warm your feeling is toward that group. On the other hand, if you don't feel very favorable toward a group—that is, if you don't care much for them—then you would place them somewhere between 0 and 50 degrees. Remember, 50 degrees means you feel neutral toward the group."

The missing data value is 99. for each thermometer.

1. Women's Liberation Movement
2. Moral Majority
3. Blacks

In order to reflect ideological dimensions, scores on the *Women's Liberation Movement* thermometer and the *Blacks* thermometer were recoded as follows:

    0 = liberal response (60 through 100)
    1 = moderate response (50)
    2 = conservative response (1 through 40)

The Moral Majority thermometer was recoded as follows:

    0 = liberal response (0 through 40)
    1 = moderate response (50)
    2 = conservative response (60 through 100)

The index was constructed by adding the three items together and then recoding the 0 through 6 range of scores to 0 through 100: 0 equals the most liberal, 100 the most conservative score.

In *1984* this index was constructed from five thermometer items. The stem was the same as in 1980.

1. Women's Liberation Movement
2. Moral Majority
3. Gay Rights
4. Pro-Life Groups
5. Blacks

The missing data value is 99 for each thermometer.

In order to reflect ideological dimensions, scores on the *Women's Liberation Movement*, *Blacks*, and *Gay Rights* thermometers were recoded as follows:

    0 = liberal response (60 through 100)
    1 = moderate response (50)
    2 = conservative response (1 through 40)

The *Moral Majority* and *Pro-Life Groups* thermometer was recoded as follows:

    0 = liberal response (0 through 40)
    1 = moderate response (50)
    2 = conservative response (60 through 100)

The index was constructed by adding the five items together and then recoding the 0 through 10 range of scores to 0 through 100: 0 equals the most liberal, 100 the most conservative score.

B. Mass Samples

In *1980* this index was constructed from three feeling thermometer items, each of which had a range of responses from 0 through 100. The stem for each item read as follows:

"I'd like to get your feelings toward some of our political leaders and other people who are in the news these days. I'll read the name of the person and I'd like you to rate that person, using this feeling thermometer. You may use any number from 0 to 100 for rating. Ratings between 50 degrees and 100 degrees mean that you feel favorable and warm toward the person. Ratings betwen 0 and 50 degrees mean that you don't feel too favorable toward the person. If we come to a person whose name you don't recognize, you don't need to rate that person. Just tell me and we'll move on to the next one. If you do recognize the name but don't feel particularly warm or cold toward the person, you would rate the person at the 50-degree mark. . . . And still using the same thermometer, how would you rate the following?"

    1. Blacks
    2. Women's Liberation Movement
    3. Evangelical Groups

The missing data values for each thermometer are 998 and 999.

In order to reflect ideological dimensions, scores on the

Women's Liberation Movement and *Blacks* thermometers
were recoded as follows:
  0 = liberal response (56 through 100)
  1 = moderate response (46 through 55)
  2 = conservative response (0 through 45)
The *Evangelical Groups* thermometer was recoded as follows:
  0 = liberal response (1 through 45)
  1 = moderate response (46 through 55)
  2 = conservative response (56 through 100)
The index was constructed by adding the three items together
and then recoding the 0 through 6 range of scores to 0 through
100: 0 equals the most liberal, 100 the most conservative
score.
In *1984* this index was constructed from five thermometer
items. The stem for these items read as follows:
"I'd like to get your feelings toward some of our political
leaders and other people who are in the news these days. I
will use something we call the feeling thermometer, and here
is how it works. I'll read the name of a person and I'd like
you to rate that person, using the feeling thermometer. Ratings between 50 degrees and 100 degrees mean that you feel
favorable and warm toward the person. Ratings between 0
degrees and 50 degrees mean that you don't care too much
for the person. You would rate the person at the 50-degree
mark if you don't feel particularly warm or cold toward the
person. If we come to a person whose name you don't recognize, you don't need to rate that person. Just tell me and
we'll move on to the next one. . . . And still using the thermometer, how would you rate the following?
1. Women's Liberation Movement
2 Evangelical Groups
3. Gay Men and Lesbians
4. Anti-Abortionists
5. Blacks
The missing data values for each thermometer are 997, 998,
999.
In order to reflect ideological dimensions, scores on the
Women's Liberation Movement, Gay Men and Lesbians, and
Blacks thermometers were recoded as follows:

0 = liberal response (56 through 100)
1 = moderate response (46 through 55)
2 = conservative response (0 through 45)

The *Evangelical Groups* and *Anti-Abortionist* thermometers were recoded as follows:

0 = liberal response (1 through 45)
1 = moderate response (46 through 55)
2 = conservative response (56 through 100)

The index was constructed by adding the five items together and then recoding the 0 through 10 range of scores to 0 through 100: 0 equals the most liberal, 100 the most conservative score.

VI. Traditional Group Index
   A. Elite Samples
      In both *1980* and *1984* this index was created from six items. The stem of these items was the same as that used in the 1980 elite sample for the construction of the social issues groups index. Six feeling thermometers were used:
      1. Conservatives
      2. Union Leaders
      3. Liberals
      4. Business Interests
      5. Democrats
      6. Republicans
      The missing data value for each thermometer is 99.
      In order to reflect ideological dimensions, scores on the *Conservatives*, *Business Interests*, and *Republicans* thermometers were recoded as follows:

      0 = liberal response (0 through 40)
      1 = moderate response (50)
      2 = conservative response (60 through 100)

      The *Union Leaders, Liberals*, and *Democrats* thermometers were recoded as follows:

      0 = liberal response (60 through 100)
      1 = moderate response (50)
      2 = conservative response (0 through 40)

      The index was constructed by adding the six items together and then recoding the 0 through 12 range of scores to 0 through 100: 0 equals the most liberal, 100 the most conservative score.

B. Mass Sample

In both *1980* and *1984* this index was constructed from six feeling thermometer items. The stem of these items is the same as was used in the 1980 mass sample for items included in the social issues groups index.

1. Conservatives
2. Labor Unions
3. Liberals
4. Business Interests
5. Democrats
6. Republicans

The missing data values for each thermometer are 998, 999 in 1980 and 997, 998, 999 in 1984.

In order to reflect ideological dimensions, scores on the *Conservatives*, *Business Interests*, and *Republicans* thermometers were recoded as follows:

0 = liberal response (0 through 45)
1 = moderate response (46 through 55)
2 = conservative response (56 through 100)

The *Labor Unions*, *Liberals*, and *Democrats* thermometers were recoded as follows:

0 = liberal response (56 through 100)
1 = moderate response (46 through 55)
2 = conservative response (0 through 45)

The index was constructed by adding the six items together and then recoding the 0 through 12 range of scores to 0 through 100: 0 equals the most liberal, 100 the most conservative score.

The index was constructed in the same manner as the elite index.

Appendix C.
Index Construction:
Measures of Political
Variables among Elites

The following measures were used to subdivide Democratic and Republican elites.

I. Strength of Party Support
    In both *1980* and *1984* Democratic and Republican elites were asked to respond to the following seven-point item:
    "Please choose the number that best describes how strongly you support your political party."
    1   not very strongly
    4   midpoint
    7   very strongly
    8, 9 missing data
    Weak Democrats and Republicans were those who responded within the range of 1 through 5. Strong Democrats and Republicans responded with a 6 or 7. The result was four categories of elite partisans:
    1   strong Democrats
    2   weak Democrats
    3   weak Republicans
    4   strong Republicans

II. Importance of Party at the Convention
    In *1980* and *1984* this index was constructed from three items. In both years the wording of the items was the same. In 1984 an introductory sentence (in brackets below) was included with the stem portion.
    "[All of you have attended *at least* one National Presidential

Nominating Convention.] In thinking about decisions that are made at conventions, which positions do you favor and which do you oppose?"

(1)   counting service to the party heavily in nominating candidates

(2)   working to minimize disagreement within the party

(3)   minimizing the role of the party organization in nominating candidates for office?

The range of responses for each item was as follows:

1   strongly favor
2   favor
3   oppose
4   strongly oppose
5   no position
8, 9 missing data

Responses were recoded to reflect the degree of importance elites attached to their party at their conventions. Items 1 and 2 were recoded as follows:

2 = high importance (1, 2)
1 = moderate (5)
0 = low importance (3, 4)

Item 3 was recoded as follows:

2 = high importance (3, 4)
1 = moderate (5)
0 = low importance (1, 2)

The index was constructed by adding together the three items and then recoding as follows:

1 = high importance (4, 5, 6)
2 = moderate (2, 3)
3 = low importance (0, 1)

III.   Strength of Local party Organization

In *1984* local party strength was assessed from responses to the following question:

"Is the party organization in your local community (city, town) very strong (1), fairly strong (2), not very strong (3), or not strong at all (4)?" Missing data values are 8, 9.

This variable was recoded as follows:

1 = strong (1, 2)
2 = weak (3, 4)

IV. Importance of Issues at the Convention

In *1980* and *1984* this index was created from three items. The stem was the same as for Measure II.

(1)   standing firm for a position even if it means resigning from the party

(2)   playing down some issues if it will improve the chances of winning

(3)   selecting a nominee who is strongly committed to the issues

The range of responses for each item was as follows:

1   strongly favor
2   favor
3   oppose
4   strongly oppose
5   no position
8, 9 missing data

Responses were recoded as follows:

Items 1 and 3 (1, 2 = 2), (5 = 1), (3, 4 = 0)
Item 2 (3, 4 = 2), (5 = 1), (1, 2 = 0)

The items were then added together and recoded so that

1 = high (4, 5, 6)
2 = moderate (2, 3)
3 = low (0, 1)

V. Partisan Competition

In *1984* local partisan competition was determined using the following question (in conjunction with elite party identification):

"How would you describe party competition within your local precinct or ward (whichever is the smaller district in your community)?"

1   very competitive—balance between the parties
2   somewhat competitive—favoring Republican party
3   somewhat competitive—favoring Democratic Party
4   noncompetitive—Republican Party dominant
5   noncompetitive—Democratic Party dominant
8, 9 missing data

The competitiveness variable was created as follows:

1 = Democratic respondent; competition favors Republican party (2 or 4 above)

2 = Democratic respondent; competition is balanced (1 above)

3 = Democratic respondent; competition favors Democratic party (3 or 5 above)

4 = Republican respondent; competition favors Democratic party (3 or 5 above)

5 = Republican respondent; competition is balanced (1 above)

6 = Republican respondent; and competition favors Republican party (2 or 4 above)

VI. Mode of Selection and Delegate Classification
In *1980* and *1984* Democratic and Republican elites were subdivided into those selected as delegates as a result of primaries and those selected by other means. In both years this subdivision was based upon the following item:
"When you were selected as a delegate to the National Convention, how were you selected?"

1   as a direct result of a primary
2   as a direct result of a state or district convention or caucus
3   by a meeting of other delegates from your state
4   by a preexisting party committee
5*   as one of the Super Delegates for public or party positions
8, 9 missing data
      *In 1980 (for Democrats only) this response read: "as one of the guaranteed 'add-on' delegates for public and party positions."

In both years responses were recoded in each party to create four groups:

1   Democrats—"primary" delegates
2   Democrats—"nonprimary" delegates
3   Republicans—"primary" delegates
4   Republicans—"nonprimary" delegates

VII. District or Other Classification
In *1980* and *1984* elites were asked: "What was your official classification as a delegate in 1984?"

1   District Delegate
2   At Large Delegate
3   Party Official/Elected Officeholder

8, 9 missing data
Democrats and Republicans were then subdivided:
1   those who were district delegates (1 above)
2   others (2, and 3 above)

VIII. District-Primary Status: 1980/1984
Based upon the "district" item and the "primary" item, a new
measure was constructed. For Democrats and Republicans the
following five classifications were developed:
1   primary, district delegates
2   primary, not district delegates
3   district, not primary delegates
4   not district, not primary delegates
5   Super Delegates (from Variable VII, response 3)
8, 9 missing data

IX. Role Preference
In *1980* and *1984* elites responded to the following question:
"During the conventions [in 1984 the question begins: 'During
the 1984 convention'] you may have been asked to make some
"important decisions. What was your approach, in general, to
decision-making? On a scale of 1 to 7, with '1' being 'vote
the way I believe is right, regardless of what the people I
represent believe,' and '7' being 'vote the way these people
would vote if they were here, regardless of what I believe,'
where would you place yourself in regard to your role as a
delegate decision-maker?" Missing data codes were 8, 9.
Responses were recoded to create the following six groups:
1   Democrat with trustee orientation (1, 2)
2   Democrat with mixed role orientation (3, 4, 5)
3   Democrat with instructed/mandated delegate role ori-
     entation (6, 7)
4   Republican with trustee orientation (1, 2)
5   Republican with mixed role orientation (3, 4, 5)
6   Republican with instructed/mandated delegate role ori-
     entation (6, 7)

X.   Campaign Focus
In *1980* and *1984* Republican and Democratic elites were subdivided into those whose campaign focus was either: (1) party,

(2) issues, or (3) a candidate. A new variable was created from three items.

"We are interested in knowing the reasons for your political involvement in recent election periods. For each campaign in which you were involved, please indicate how much of your activity was motivated by commitments to the party, to the candidate, or to an issue position or special group. If you were not at all involved in the campaign, please indicate this in the first column."

1   I was committed to party work
2   I wanted to help a particular candidate
3   I wanted to work for one issue or for some specific group

Responses to each item were as follows:

1   a lot
2   some
3   none
0   not involved in the campaign
8, 9 missing data

The "focus" item was then constructed as follows:

1   Party focus: item 1 = 1, item 2 ≠ 1, item 3 ≠ 1)
2   candidate focus: item 2 = 1, item 1 ≠ 1, item 3 ≠ 1)
3   issue focus: item 3 = 1 and
     a) item 1 ≠ 1 and item 2 ≠ 1 or
     b) item 1 = 1 and item 2 ≠ 1 or
     c) item 1 ≠ 1 and item 2 = 1

XI. Convention Representation
     This measure was constructed in *1980* and *1984* by recoding the following item:
     "Which groups listed below come closest to describing the ones you represented at the [1984] convention? Please rank the groups in order of importance to you with the first as the most important and so on."
     In both years this item was recoded as follows:
     1   party (code = 1)
     2   candidate (code = 2)
     3   voter (code = 3)
     4   social issues (code = 10, 13, 19, 20, 25, 33, 39, 50, 55, 58, 59, 60, 65, 66, 67, 69, 86)

5   mainstream politics (code = 21, 26, 27, 28, 40-45, 49,
       72, 79, 80, 81, 82, 83, 85, 87, 89, 90-97)
00, 88, 99   missing data

XII. Delegate's Sponsor
      This measure was constructed in *1980* and *1984* by recoding
      the following item:
      "When you were being selected as a delegate, did you get help
      from the following groups? Please rank the groups in order of
      importance to your selection with the first as the most important
      and so on."
      The item was recoded as follows:
      1   party (1980, code = 3; 1984, code = 1)
      2   candidate (1980, code = 4; 1984, code = 2)
      3   voter (1980, code = 2; 1984, code = 3)
      4   social issues (both years, code = 10 13, 19, 20, 25,
             33, 39, 50, 55, 58, 59, 60, 65, 66, 67, 69, 86)
      5   mainstream politics (both years, code = 21, 26, 27,
             28, 40-45, 49, 72, 79, 80, 81, 82, 83, 85, 87, 89, 90-
             97)
      00, 88, 99   missing data

XIII. Party Leadership Wings
       In *1984* the feeling thermometers listed below were used to
       create variables that reflect leadership wings within both par-
       ties.

Among Democrats	*Among Republicans*
W. Mondale	R. Reagan
L. Johnson	G. Bush
H. Humphrey	R. Dole
J. Carter	G. Ford
G. McGovern	R. Nixon
G. Ferraro	B. Goldwater
E. Kennedy	J. Kemp
J. Jackson	D. Eisenhower

         0 = cold
       100 = hot
       999 = md (missing data)

The following program was used to create the leadership wings within both parties:

(1) For Democrats:

Compute Demf1 = (Mondale + Johnson + Humphrey + Carter)/4

Compute Demf2 = (McGovern + Ferraro + Kennedy + Johnson)/4

Compute score1 = (Demf1 − Demf2)

If (Demf2 lt 50) Dwing = 1

If (Demf2 ge 50 and score1 ge 10) Dwing = 2

If (Demf2 ge 50 and score1 le 70) Dwing = 3

If (Demf2 ge 50 and [score1 gt − 10 and score1 lt 10]) Dwing = 4

If Sysmis (Demf1) Dwing = 5

If Sysmis (Demf2) Dwing = 5

As a result, the Democratic leadership wing variable has the following values:

1   liberal party wing rated at 50 or lower
2   mainstream wing favored over the liberal wing by 10 points
3   liberal wing favored over the mainstream wing by 10 points
4   all other Democrats for whom there were responses
5   Democrats with missing data codes on the thermometers

(2) For Republicans:

Compute Repf1 = (Reagan + Bush + Dole + Ford)/4

Compute Repf2 = (Nixon + Goldwater + Kemp + Eisenhower)/4

Compute Score2 = (Repf1 − Repf2)

If (Score2 le − 10) Rwing = 1

If (Score2 ge − 7.50 and score 2 le 7.50) Rwing = 2

If (Score2 ge 10) Rwing = 3

As a result, the Republican leadership wing variable has the following values:

1   most conservative party wing
2   middle group
3   moderate wing

XIV. Party Ideological Factions

In *1984* ideological factions within each party were determined as follows:

Within each party the elite liberal/conservative self-placement variable (V2142) was recoded as follows:

V2142 1 = liberal − 7 = conservative

Recode V2142 (1, 2 = 1) (3 = 3) (4 = 4) (5 = 5) (6, 7 = 7)

For *Democrats*: the variable locating other Democrats at the convention on the liberal/conservative scale (V2156) was recoded in two ways:

Compute Ddels1 = V2156

Compute Ddels2 = V2156

Recode Ddels1 (1 thru 4 = 1) (5 thru 7 = 2)/
       Ddels2 (1 thru 3 = 1) (4 thru 7 = 2)

The Democratic ideological factions were then determined by using a combination of the self-location variable and the other location variables as follows:

1   liberal: (a) V2142 = 1 or
           (b) V2142 = 3 and Ddels 1 = 2

2   moderate: (a) V2142 = 4 or
           (b) V2142 = 3 and Ddels1 = 1 or
           (c) V2142 = 5 and Ddels2 = 2

3   conservative: (a) V2142 = 7 or
           (b) V2142 = 5 and Ddels2 = 1

For *Republicans*, the same procedure was followed. First the liberal/conservative location of other Republicans (V2155) was recoded in two ways.

Compute RDels1 = V2155

Compute RDels2 = V2155

Recode RDels1 (1 thru 4 = 1) (5, 6, 7 = 2)/RDels2 (1, 2, 3 = 1) (4 thru 7 = 2)

The Republican ideological factions were then determined by using a combination of self- and other ideological placement:

1   liberal: (a) V2142 = 1 or
           (b)   V2142 = 3 and RDels
           1 = 2

2   moderate: (a) V2142 = 4 or
                 (b)   V2142 = 3   and
                 RDels1 = 1 or
                 (c)   V2142 = 5   and
                 RDels2 = 2
3   conservative: (a) V2142 = 7 or
                    (b)   V2142 = 5 and
                    RDels2 = 1

Notes

Preface

1. V.O. Key, Jr., *Public Opinion and American Democracy* (New York: Alfred A. Knopf, 1961), 536.
2. Ibid., 536-37, 551.

1. The Study of Presidential Politics in America

1. Warren E. Miller and J. Merrill Shanks, "Policy Directions and Presidential Leadership: Alternative Interpretation of the 1980 Presidential Election," *British Journal of Political Science* 12 (1982): 299-356; J. Merrill Shanks and Warren E. Miller, "Policy Directions and Performance Evaluations: Complementary Explanations of the Reagan Elections" (paper presented at annual meeting of American Political Science Association, New Orleans, La., 1985); Morris P. Fiorina, *Retrospective Voting in American National Elections* (New Haven, Conn.: Yale Univ. Press, 1981).
2. Martin P. Wattenburg, *The Decline of American Political Parties: 1952-1984* (Cambridge, Mass.: Harvard Univ. Press, 1986).
3. Fiorina, *Retrospective Voting*; Donald R. Kinder, "Presidents, Prosperity, and Public Opinion," *Public Opinion Quarterly* 45 (1981): 1-21; Donald R. Kinder, Gordon S. Adams, and Paul W. Gronke, "Economics and Politics in 1984" (paper delivered at annual meeting of American Political Science Association, New Orleans, La., 1985); Donald R. Kinder and D.R. Kiewiet, "Economic Discontents and Political Behavior: The Role of Personal Grievances and Collective Economic Judgements in Congressional Voting," *American Journal of Political Science* 23 (1979): 495-527; Donald R. Kinder and D.R. Kiewiet, "Sociotropic Politics," *British Journal of Political Science* 2 (1981): 129-61; Donald R. Kinder and W.R. Mebane, Jr., "Politics and Economics in Everyday Life," in *The Political Process and Economic Change*, ed. K. Monroe (New York: Agathon, 1983); John H. Kessel, Presidential Parties (Homewood, Ill.: Dorsey Press, 1984); Warren E. Miller and Theresa E. Levitin, *Leadership and Change: Presidential*

Elections 1952-1976 (Cambridge, Mass.: Winthrop, 1976); Herbert Asher, *Presidential Elections and American Politics: Voters, Candidates, and Campaigns since 1952* (Homewood, Ill.: Dorsey Press, 1984); D.R. Kiewiet, *Macroeconomics and Micropolitics: The Electoral Effects of Economic Issues* (Chicago: Univ. of Chicago Press, 1984); Edward R. Tufte, *Political Control of the Economy* (Princeton, N.J.: Princeton Univ. Press, 1980); Edward R. Tufte, "Determinants of the Outcomes of Midterm Congressional Elections," *American Political Science Review* 69 (1975): 812-26.

    4. Warren E. Miller and M. Kent Jennings, *Parties in Transition: A Longitudinal Study of Party Elites and Party Supporters* (New York: Russell Sage Foundation, 1986).

    5. Richard Fenno, *Home Style: House Members in Their Districts* (Boston: Little, Brown, 1978).

    6. Jeane Kirkpatrick, *The New Presidential Elite: Men and Women in National Politics* (New York: Russell Sage Foundation and Twentieth Century Fund, 1976); Jeane Kirkpatrick, "Representation in American National Conventions: The Case of 1972," *British Journal of Political Science* 5, no. 3 (1975): 265-322; Herbert McClosky, Paul J. Hoffman, and Rosemary O'Hara, "Issue Conflict and Consensus among Party Leaders and Followers," *American Political Science Review* 54 (1960): 406-27; Miller and Jennings, *Parties in Transition*; Dennis G. Sullivan, "Party Unity: Appearance and Reality," *Political Science Quarterly* 92 (Winter 1977-78): 635-45; John S. Jackson III, "Political Party Leaders and the Mass Public: 1980-1984" (paper presented at annual meeting of Midwest Political Science Association, Chicago, 1985); John S. Jackson III, Jesse C. Brown, and Barbara L. Brown, "Recruitment, Representation, and Political Values," *American Politics Quarterly* 6, no. 2 (1973): 187-212; Norman R. Luttbeg, ed., "Political Linkage in a Large Society," in *Public Opinion and Public Policy* (Homewood, Ill.: Dorsey Press, 1974); John S. Jackson III, Barbara Leavitt Brown, and David Bositis, "Herbert McClosky and Friends Revisited," *American Politics Quarterly* 10, no. 2 (1982): 158-80.

    7. John H. Kessel, *Presidential Parties*; Leon D. Epstein, *Political Parties in the American Mold* (Madison: Univ. of Wisconsin Press, 1986); Frank J. Sorauf, *Party Politics in America* (Boston: Little, Brown, 1984); Samuel J. Eldersveld, *Political Parties: A Behavioral Analysis* (Chicago: Rand McNally, 1964).

    8. James L. Gibson, Cornelius P. Cotter, John F. Bibbey, and Robert J. Huckshorn, *Party Organizations in American Politics* (New York: Praeger, 1984); William Crotty, *Decision for the Democrats: Reforming the Party Structure* (Baltimore, Md.: John Hopkins Univ. Press, 1978); William Crotty, *Party Reform* (New York: Longman, 1983); David R. Mayhew, *Placing Parties in American Politics* (Princeton, N.J.: Princeton Univ. Press,

1986); Nelson W. Polsby and Aaron Wildavsky, *Presidential Elections: Strategies of American Electoral Politics*, 6th ed. (New York: Scribner, 1984).

9. Polsby and Wildavsky, *Presidential Elections*.

10. McClosky, Hoffman, and O'Hara, "Issue Conflict and Consensus"; Kirkpatrick, *The New Presidential Elite*; Jackson, "Political Party Leaders and the Mass Public"; Jackson, Brown, and Brown, "Recruitment, Representation, and Political Values"; Jackson, Brown, and Bositis, "Herbert McClosky and Friends Revisited"; Sullivan, "Party Unity"; Miller and Jennings, *Parties in Transition*.

11. A major exception is provided by Kirkpatrick, *The New Presidential Elite*.

12. Ibid.

13. McClosky, Hoffman, and O'Hara, "Issue Conflict and Consensus."

14. Miller and Jennings, *Parties in Transition*.

15. Thomas Amlie, *Let's Look at the Record* (Madison, Wis.: Capital City Press, 1950).

2. Partisan Polarization and Factionalism, 1980 and 1984

1. Ellis Sandoz, "The Silent Majority Finds Its Voice," in *Election 84: Landslide without a Mandate*, ed. Ellis Sandoz and Cecil V. Crabb (New York: New American Library, 1985); Hamilton Jordan, "What the Democrats Must Do," *Newsweek* 104, no. 22 (1984): 60; John W. Mashek and Joseph P. Shapiro, "What Defeat Taught the Democrats," *U.S. News and World Report* 97, no. 21 (1984): 38.

2. Shanks and Miller, "Policy Directions and Performance Evaluations"; Warren E. Miller, "A New Context for Presidential Politics: The Reagan Legacy," *Political Behavior* 9 (1987): 2; Thomas Ferguson and Joel Rogers, "The Myth of America's Turn to the Right," *Atlantic Monthly* 257, no. 5 (1986): 43-53; Barry Sussman, "What's the Evidence for This Shift to the Right We Hear About?" *Washington Post Weekly*, July 21, 1986, 37.

3. Miller and Jennings, *Parties in Transition*.

3. Mass-Elite Similarities

1. McClosky, Hoffman, and O'Hara, "Issue Conflict and Consensus."

2. Kirkpatrick, *The New Presidential Elite*.

3. Miller and Jennings, *Parties in Transition*.

4. Linkage Mechanisms: Party

1. It should be remembered that 1984 attitudes toward domestic spending provided the only instance in which the ideological position of a group of rank-and-file followers was *more* extreme than the position taken by their party elites.

2. It is important to note that these conclusions are supported by the correlational measures of dissimilarity displayed in the table, by the differences of means for our national aggregations of individual elite mass participants, *and* by the comparison of mean differences of state-based mass and elite means. That is to say, state by state, the differences between elite mean score and mean scores for state partisan masses were *greater* for issue-oriented elites than for all others. This constitutes an important confirmation of the validity of our correlational measure of group diferences. It should also be noted that the domestic spending issue provided the single instance in which the Democratic rank and file was more "liberal" than the Democratic elite and, therefore, probably more like the more liberal elite activists.

3. Robert Weissberg, "Collective vs. Dyadic Representation in Congress," *American Political Science Review* 72 (1978): 535-47.

4. Warren E. Miller and Donald E. Stokes, "Constituency Influence in Congress," *American Political Science Review* 57 (1963): 45-56; Donald E. Stokes and Warren E. Miller, "Party Government and the Saliency of Congress," in Angus Campbell, Phillip E. Converse, Warren E. Miller, and Donald E. Stokes, *Elections and the Political Order* (New York: Wiley, 1966); Warren E. Miller, "Majority Rule and the Representative System of Government" in *Cleavages, Ideologies and Party Systems: Contributions to Comparative Political Sociology*, ed. E. Allardt and Y. Littunen (Helsinki: Transactions of the Westermarck Society, 1964).

5. Phillip E. Converse and Roy Pierce, *Political Representation in France* (Cambridge, Mass.: Harvard Univ. Press, 1986).

6. Weissberg, "Collective vs. Dyadic Representation."

7. Christopher Achen, "Measuring Representation," *American Journal of Political Science* 22 (1978): 475-510; idem, "Measuring Representation: Perils of the Regression Coefficient," *American Political Science Review* 21 (1977): 805-15.

8. Miller, "Majority Rule and the Representative System of Government."

5. Linkage Mechanisms: Ideological Factions and Issue Representation

1. Miller and Jennings, *Parties in Transition.*
2. Miller and Shanks, "Policy Directions and Presidential Leadership"; Shanks and Miller, "Policy Directions and Performance Evaluations."

6. Linkage Mechanisms: Political Leadership

1. Daniel Bell, *The End of Ideology* (Glencoe, Ill.: Free Press, 1960).
2. Miller and Jennings, *Parties in Transition.*

7. Linkage Mechanisms: Elite Orientations

1. Kirkpatrick, *The New Presidential Elite.*
2. This, of course, excepts the seminal work of McClosky some thirty years earlier; see McClosky, Hoffman, and O'Hara, "Issue Conflict and Consensus."
3. Harvey Mansfield, Jr., notes that "medieval representation used 'representative machinery' to secure consent. But 'representative government' is government that uses representative machinery because it is authorized solely and entirely by consent." Harvey Mansfield, Jr. "Modern and Medieval Representation," in *Representation*, Nomos X, ed. J. Roland Pennock and John W. Chapman (New York: Atherton Press, 1968), 78.
4. "Of course, these concepts were not always associated with the theory or practice of representation. Representative institutions were initially established by strong governments who sought the help—usually financial—of notable citizens." In Charles Beard's words, "It began its career as an instrument of power and convenience in the hands of the state": Charles A. Beard, "The Teutonic Origins of Representative Government," *American Political Science Review* 26 (1932): 44. See also A.H. Birch, *Representative and Responsible Government* (Toronto: Univ. of Toronto Press, 1964), 1; Charles A. Beard and John D. Lewis, "Representative Government in Evolution," *American Political Science Review* 26 (1932): 223-40.
5. Kirkpatrick, *The New Presidential Elite*, pp. 283-84.
6. See Nelson W. Polsby, "The Democratic Nomination," in *The American Elections of 1980*, ed. Austin Ranney (Washington, D.C.: American Enterprise Institute, 1981); James Lengles and Byron Shafer, "Primary Rules, Political Power, and Social Change," *American Political Science Review* 70 (March 1976): 25-40; Kirkpatrick, *Representation in American National Conventions: The Case of 1972.*

7. Kirkpatrick, *The New Presidential Elite*, 285.

8. Heinz Eulau, "The Congruence Model Revisited," *Legislative Studies Quarterly* 12, no. 2 (1987): 171-214, criticizes this limited conception from a variety of perspectives, not the least of which focuses on such larger or lesser interventions as those of ombudsman or pork-barrel provider.

Index

abortion, 17, 19, 27, 29, 78
  See also issues: social
Achen, Christopher, 66, 67, 68, 174
  n 7
Adams, Gordon S., 171 n 3
affirmative action, 78
  See also issues: social
agriculture, 78
  See also issues
Allardt, E., 174 n 4
American Voter, The (Miller and
  Stokes), xi, xiii
Amlie, Thomas, 173 n 15
Anderson, John, 101
Asher, Herbert, 172 n 3

Baker, Howard, 101
Beard, Charles A., 175 n 4
Bell, Daniel, 175 n 6.1
Bibbey, John F., 172 n 8
Birch, A.H., 175 n 4
blacks, attitudes to, 10, 17, 19, 27,
  29
Bositis, David, 172 n 6, 173 n 10
Brennan, Nancy, xiv
Brown, Barbara Leavitt, 172 n 6,
  173 n 10
Brown, Jesse C., 172 n 6, 173 n 10
Bush, George, 90, 93, 101
busing, 17, 19, 27, 28, 29, 101
  See also issues: social

campaigns
  consultants in, 1

funding of, 1
mass-elite similarities in, 31-46
  See also issues; *parties by name*
Campbell, Angus, 174 n 4
candidates
  black, 90
  and convention delegates, 6, 8,
    12, 55-57, 59, 77, 90-98,
    110-11, 113-14
  and mass-elite linkages, 90, 136
  packaging of, 1
  vs. parties, 2, 132
  personalities of, 3
  and political parties, 60, 89, 132
  and reform, 107
  women, 90
  See also issues; leadership, political
Carter, Jimmy, 13, 20, 25, 26, 45
  centrism of, 38, 91, 113, 133
  conservative support for, 19, 21,
    22
  1980 nomination of, 99, 101, 105
Center for Political Studies, xii, xv
Center for the American Woman in
  Politics (Rutgers University),
  xiv
Chapman, John W., 175 n 3
Cold War, 89
conservatives, 7, 11, 20, 35, 36
  and Democratic party, 13, 19, 53,
    83-85, 91-92, 93, 103
  and Republican party, 13-14, 17,
    21, 22, 53, 74, 79-80, 83-85,
    93, 95, 116, 133